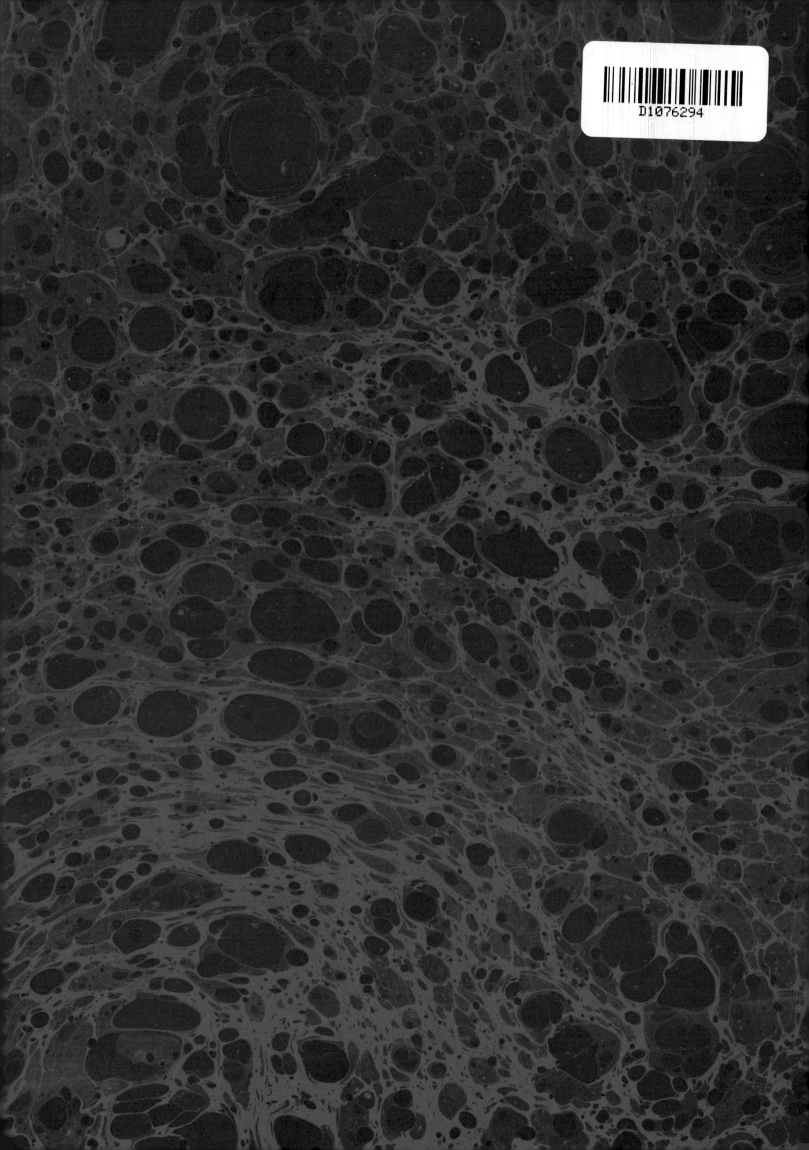

The Enchanted World

GHOSTS

The Enchanted World

GHOSTS

by the Editors of Time-Life Books

The Content

Time-Life Books · Amsterdam

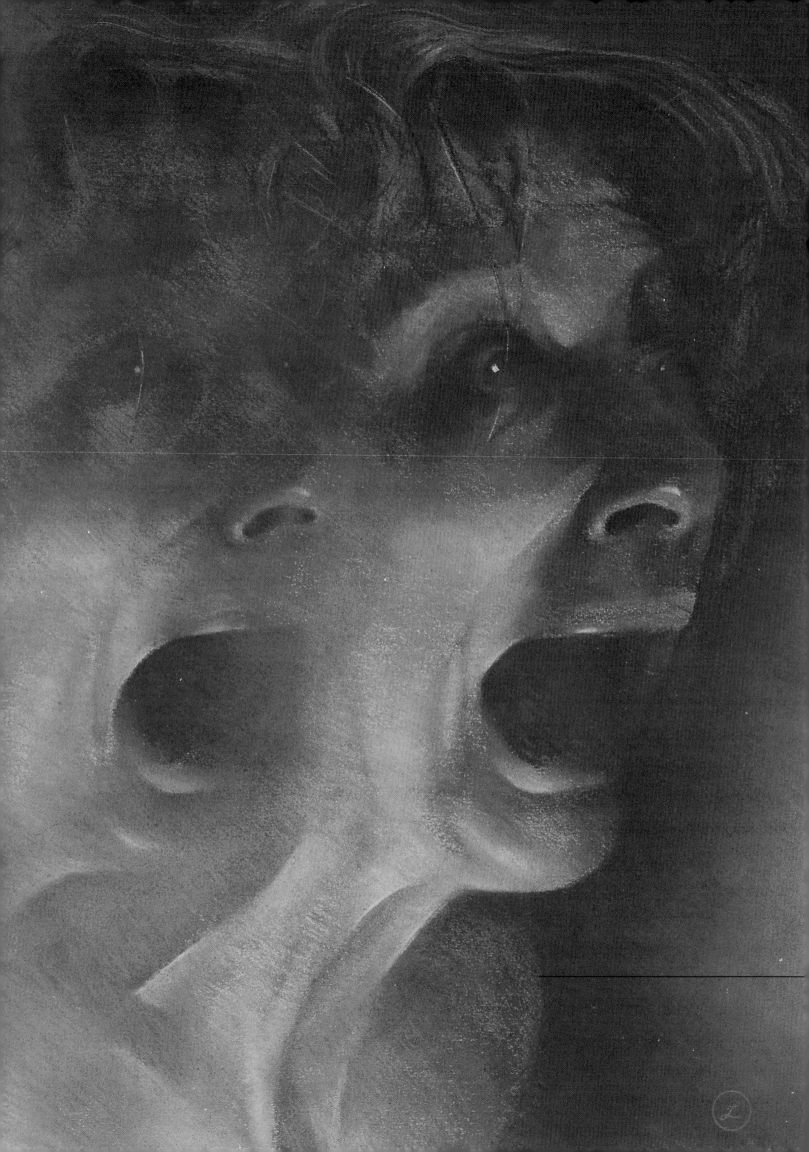

Chapter One

Guises of the Reaper

Late one spring night in the last century, a certain Englishman found himself, to his astonishment, standing in the garden outside his house. It was quite bewildering. He remembered falling asleep in his bed, but he had no memory of waking and walking out the door. Yet here he was, shivering in the chill, his bare feet buried in rain-soaked grass. Another surprise awaited him: When he tried the door, it proved to be locked.

The moon had set, and the familiar garden had become a foreign landscape painted in shades of black and gray. His prized privet hedge was an anonymous, hump-backed blur, larger than it looked by daylight; the still-bare branches of the trees were skeletal arms stretched wide against the stars. But from the window of his wife's bedroom, light shone warm and welcoming into the night. He made for the window at once. His wife could be trusted to admit him to the house without the usual jokes reserved for wandering sleepwalkers.

His wife's bed was directly opposite the window, and he observed with some disapproval that she had fallen asleep while the candles still burned. What disturbed him more was the unnatural effect of the candle flames. Her face, sunk among mounds of pillows, looked old and sallow; her hands, curled upon the counterpane, seemed parchmented by age.

Not wishing to frighten his wife by knocking, he stepped close to the panes and stared, concentrating all his will upon her to make her awake and see him there. Obedient even in sleep, she stirred and sat up. Her eyes focused on the window, looking directly into his own, and he gave a benign and reassuring smile.

The result was not what he had hoped. For a moment, his wife did nothing. Then her head began to bob like that of an automaton, back and forth on a straining neck. Her eyes widened and bulged; her mouth opened, the lips drawn back tight. She screamed, as those in nightmares scream, without a sound.

Unnerved, he took a step backward. His wife found her voice, and her shriek rent the air and battered the windowpane. It went crazily on and on, punctuated by hoarse and gasping breaths, rising and falling and rising again. He raised his arm and knocked upon the windowpane to put an end to the appalling noise.

He saw a curious sight then. He saw it quite clearly and all at once: the gleaming white bones of his forearm, neatly articulated to the bones of his wrist; the pebbly joints of his five fingers loosely bound by frayed strings of ligament; and the fluttering shreds of his own winding sheet. Then darkness and nothingness swallowed him once again.

If truth be told, no mortal knows with certainty just what he saw or thought that night, or where he went after he disappeared or even who he was. But the woman had no doubts about the identity of her visitor, and with the instinctive sympathy of the long-married, she felt sure she could guess what was in his mind. The grinning skeleton who plaintively tapped at her window could only have been her husband, risen from the grave where he had rested for many years and somehow compelled to return to home and hearth.

He had joined, it seemed, the storied legions of the restless dead, those ghosts of men and women who, although no longer of this world, have yet to find peace in another. In centuries past (and even now, although the present age is less hospitable to them), members of the spirit company frequently appeared among mortals. They came in an infinity of guises and for a multitude of reasons. Some manifested themselves as nothing more than rustlings in halls, cold spots on floors or shadows in corners. Some took human form, their aspects familiar save for the ashen pallor imparted by the grave and a frightening, elusive insubstantiality. They appeared and disappeared at random: Existing as they did in another dimension, the barriers of the ordinary world—walls, roofs, floors and doors—had no meaning for them, and they passed effortlessly through solid structures.

Most disturbing of all were ghosts who came not as they had been in life, but as in death of long standing, their briefly animated corpses beribboned with tattered, earth-caked remnants of shrouds. Some,

The lantern bearer lights the way
For those who no more seize the day:
Blind eyes peer out from every head
That crowds the carriage of the dead.

maimed or mutilated at the moment of death, returned in like fashion — armless or legless or horribly headless.

As for the motives that impelled the hauntings, they evidently were as varied as those that informed the actions of the living. Some ghosts came to complete business unfinished in life; some, victims of real or fancied wrongs while living, came bent on vengeance. Some, malefactors while alive, existed in perpetual punishment, doomed to reenact their crimes forever, denied the easeful rest of death. Some returned to life because they were summoned by the living: Ghosts could be called from the grave, although only the foolhardy or careless did so. Still others did their spectral work for no apparent purpose, driven by malevolent forces terrifyingly meaningless to their living victims; it was as if they were consumed by envy of anyone still possessing the gift of life. And some ghosts were only harmless, wistful spirits, apparently unable to leave the familiar scenes of their past.

The sight of these apparitions, no matter how innocuous they might be, almost always struck terror in the hearts of the living. The fear of the dead is an age-old fear: That they should walk again seems to violate the processes of nature and deny the rules that reassure humankind of the essentially orderly structure of the universe. Moreover, a ghost is an animated *memento mori*, a distressing reminder to the living that they too will die.

"Golden lads and girls all must, as chimney sweepers, come to dust," runs the old song. Yet it is hard to accept death as life's shadow and conqueror. It is hard to believe that the body warmed by the summer sun or by comforting wintertime fires should be forever cold; that the person who lies safe and happily companioned at night should be forever alone in the dark; that the eyes that greet the world flowering in the springtime and the voice that carols in praise of it should be perpetually blinded and silenced. No matter what the joy in life, no matter how bright and shining its pleasures, the end is the same: a solitary plot of cold earth that the rain beats upon and the wind howls over. Within that patch of ground, flesh once sweet and rosy grows foul and gray and shrinks and shreds from the bones; heart and brain melt away to nothing.

That is mortality: to end alone, forever in the dark. And behind the countenance of even a smiling ghost is the cold leer of the cadaver: "Just as I am," the ghost tells the living, "so shall you be."

That message was well known in days gone by, when the world was a wilder, more dangerous place and the margins between the natural and the supernatural were not as distinct as they would later seem. People were well acquainted with the manifestations of death in life. They watched for the signs of the Reaper, so that they might be ready to meet him when the time came. Accepting the inevitable, they did not care to go to their graves unprepared or leave their world without goodbys, all dignity lost in fear.

Some signs were homely warnings, oddities in domestic life that signified the imminence of change. A clock that

stopped or chimed between the hours, disturbing the measured march of time, meant Death's eye was on the household. A guttering candle whose melting wax slid down the shaft in a broad stream—a winding-sheet shape—was another. Bees that swarmed not to fields or orchards in their quest for nectar but down chimneys into houses—so many winged souls, searching for companions—were another. A barnyard cock that crowed not at dawn but in the dead of night, breaking the seemly silence, was still another.

Birds, in fact, ranging across the countryside in flight high above roof, steeple, field and forest, easily able to see any stranger and observe any change, served as heralds of Death more than any other beasts. A bird that beat against a windowpane or, worse, flew into a house, brought grim news to those within. Owls, which hunted at night and possessed sharp eyes that saw every stealthy movement in the dark, knew when the Reaper drew near. An owl that hooted persistently near a house or tapped at the windowpane conveyed a bleak message. And the world over, the raven, with its wheeling flight and keen, intelligent eyes, was a precursor of death. The raven had served as a bird of prophecy from time immemorial. It was sacred to Apollo and the oracles in ancient Greece. In Arabia, the raven was called Abu Zájir, or "Father of Omens." In Germany, when a raven deserted its raucous flock and flew alone over a house or croaked harshly near the door, the family within prepared for grief. The British thought the bird could detect the odor of decay in a sick person even before the breath had left the body.

These all were creatures of the natural world, however, and while deviations from their usual behaviors might mean that Death was on his way, they might as easily be simple oddities with perfectly reasonable explanations. But there were other forerunners of death that lent themselves to no natural explanation and that could never be dismissed with a shrug or a show of indifference.

Such were black dogs, nightwalkers feared throughout the British Isles. The dogs that preceded death were given various names—Black Shuck in East Anglia, Skriker and Trash-hound in Lancashire, Padfoot in Yorkshire—but all were of the same fell race. They appeared on dark nights in country lanes, loping easily along, eyes searching for solitary travelers who should have been safe at home. The people of Lancashire said that as such a dog approached, it swelled and grew until it was the size of a calf, and its saucer-wide eyes glowed red in the dark, fired by malice and hunger. Those who saw the dog knew—even though it passed them with little more than a sideways glance—that their time had come.

No less eerie were the banshees that wailed for the dying throughout the British Isles and France. The name comes from the Gaelic *bean side*, meaning "woman of the fairy folk," and some banshees were indeed of fairy lineage; others, it was thought, were ghosts themselves. They seemed attached to individual families, and they mourned the coming intrusion of death into the clan. Family members might hear their terrible cries swirling around the house in the night, rising, it seemed, from the very walls and floors. Sometimes the wailing came from out of doors, and those within who looked from a window would see a rail-thin woman, her face white, her long hair streaming, her eyes blood red with weeping. She would drift in the air around the walls, peering through the windowpanes, to search for the one whose death she awaited. When she found that one and beckoned, the person had to go.

In Scotland, the banshee took another form: She was called the *bean-nighe*, or "washing woman." Small and squat—sometimes even grotesquely childlike in appearance—the *bean-nighe* was seen by travelers passing remote pools and fords. She ceaselessly beat bloodstained shrouds upon the river stones and wrung the water from the cloth, and sometimes she crooned a dirge all to herself. It was said that the traveler who dared to address her would hear the names of those about to die and would also hear—if he wished—his own fate foretold.

The *bean-nighe* was frequently described as a ghost herself—usually the ghost of a woman who had died in childbirth. This was an untimely death, a curtailment of

Nodding in the window, tapping on the stair, a fetch waited patiently for its

victim to appear. It took a living woman's shape, and when she saw it beside her, she

knew her time had come: The fetch, or double, summoned mortals to the grave.

the normal course of a life. The dead mother was doomed to be a beckoner of the living, washing the shrouds of those among them who were about to join her, until the date of what would have been her natural death had been reached.

There was another beckoner, much less obtrusive than the banshee, one not attached to Celtic countries: It appeared in every land and in every walk of life. It was a quiet creature, but its demand was inexorable, and all who saw it knew its intent. A 17th Century tale shows it at work:

The episode began late one summer afternoon in the formally patterned garden of a Kentish country house. Most of the family was away visiting a neighbor, but a daughter of the house lingered there, walking on graveled paths among the sculptured boxwood, past fragrant flower beds carefully planted to make ornamental carpets on the lawn. She walked slowly because of the heat and because her movement was restricted by the fashions of the time—lace, ribbons, ruffles and thick falls of skirt.

She glanced at the brick façade of the house, glowing in the late light. A movement caught her eye. In the dark square of a window she could see the pale oval of a face, indistinct at this distance, yet seeming to regard her steadily. It was, no doubt, a servant, idling about upstairs.

The young woman took another turn around the garden, but the afternoon was fast dimming into dusk, and from the river that coursed nearby, mist began to rise and curl gently across the lawns, bringing a chill with it. The woman went indoors.

The house seemed unnaturally quiet. In the hall, she paused, overcome by the sensation—not, of course, uncommon in an empty house—that she was being watched. Nothing was in the hall, however, save for ancestral portraits, the usual collection of bewigged gentlemen and white-haired ladies swathed in folds of gleaming fabric and attended by solemn children and arrays of lap dogs.

In the center of the hall, a great stair wound up to the second floor of the house. As the woman set her foot on the first tread, she heard a rustling high above; she looked up and saw what might have been the hem of a petticoat in the shadows of the landing. This disappeared instantly; her eyes had deceived her.

She went to her own bedchamber. It was still warm there from the sunlit day, and the air that drifted in the open windows was laden with the scents of water and earth. In the perfect stillness, she heard a rook cry harshly as it flew to its roost in the home wood.

She walked to a mirror and inspected the oval of her face. A curl had tumbled from its ribbon onto her cheek, and she raised her hand to tie it back.

Hands still in midair, she froze, watching the mirror intently. A woman had come in the door behind her. The image grew clearer as the figure approached, petticoats rustling. The intruder stopped just behind the young woman and stared into the glass. Then the newcomer shifted her gaze to the woman and moved her lips in a mechanical parody of a smile. The young woman pressed her hand to the glass: It was herself who stood beside her, exact in every physical detail. But the breast of her twin did not rise and fall with breathing, and no voice came from the pallid lips.

When the family came home later in the evening, they found the daughter on her bed, feverish, racked with pain, and clearly dying. With her last strength, the young woman whispered of the encounter, repeating the tale again and again in tones of terror. Her eyes were still bright with fear when she died.

The woman had seen the most frightening of apparitions — in Britain variously known as the double or fetch or co-walker, and in Germany called the *Doppelgänger*, or "double goer." These were spirits who could assume the physical form of those about to die. Sometimes they appeared to friends or relatives of the dying — and their mimickry was so convincing that, if they were met casually walking along the street, they might be taken for the person involved. More often, however, they delivered their silent message to that person alone. And after death occurred, it was said, the double shed the mortal image and fled to whatever world had spawned it.

Double and banshee, raven and owl, all were no more than heralds, the forerunners of the hunter of souls, hungry Death himself. He was the fearsome slayer of man, woman and child, of peasant, priest and prince alike. No one knew who he was, for he assumed many shapes and guises as he went about his business. But in every country there were names for him and tales about him.

According to Englishmen who had traveled in Arab lands, Death there took the form of a woman. A story was told of a merchant of Baghdad who was approached one day by his servant. The poor man's face was pale and his hands were shaking.

"Master," said the servant, "I saw Death in the marketplace today, a tall woman hooded in black. She looked directly at me and made a threatening gesture with her hand." The terrified menial begged for his master's horse, that he might flee to the city of Samarra and so escape the clutches of the woman Death.

The master agreed, and when the servant had left for Samarra — riding as fast as the horse could carry him — he went himself to the market place, to see whether Death would appear.

She did indeed, hooded in black as the servant had said. She idled among the stands, examining the fruits piled there; from time to time, she tapped a person on the shoulder, and that person blanched and hurried away.

The merchant beckoned her to him, and she came willingly. He asked with curiosity why she had threatened his servant.

"That was not a threatening gesture," answered Death demurely. "It was a gesture of surprise at seeing him here in Baghdad. I have an appointment with him tonight in Samarra, you see." And with a smile, she disappeared.

In Brittany, Death was a man known as the Ankou. Some said he was none other than the fratricide Cain, eldest son of Adam, who was doomed to roam the earth forever as a collector of human carrion. Others thought that he was the ghost of

In the bright heat of Baghdad, a servant shivered in the shadow of Death. The man fled to Samarra—where Death had planned to meet him all along.

the last man to die each year, coming back to fill new graves before yielding place to his successor. Most people simply accepted him as Death.

All agreed, however, about his appearance. Tall and gaunt, often wearing a wide-brimmed hat, and sometimes manifest as a whitened skeleton swathed in a ragged shroud, the Ankou was a night-stalker, emerging when prudent folk were safely indoors. He walked the lanes of the province with a peculiar, awkward gait, his head turning stiffly from side to side with each step, scenting the air, for his eye sockets were empty. The Ankou was blind. Sometimes he carried a club or a sword, sometimes he went about with a scythe slung over his shoulder. Always he was accompanied by a cart drawn by horses or oxen, which he used to carry away those he had come to claim. This betrayed his presence. Living folk in their houses could hear through the shutters the creaking of the cart wheels and the heavy footfalls of the death bringer.

Once, it was said, the Ankou could see; an eerie flame flickered in the eye sockets. But that light was snuffed out by a being more powerful than the Ankou himself.

It happened, the story goes, that Saint

Peter descended to earth and fell into step beside the Ankou and his cart. The two powerful beings walked in silence down a dirt lane bordered by hayfields. There, in the late dusk, a farmer and his servant still labored. At the sound of the cart's creaking axle, the birds ceased their singing and the farmer dropped to the ground, attempting to make himself invisible. He motioned his servant to do the same.

The servant was a simple man, however. Like most Bretons, he had a fine musical voice, and he continued to scythe the hay, singing a gay and lilting song as loudly as he could to keep up his courage.

The Ankou brought the cart to a halt, and the gaunt face turned toward the singer. "You will be dead in eight days," he said dully. But the servant only sang louder. At this challenge, the green fire blazed in the Ankou's eyes, and he turned to his companion, ready to prove his power.

But Saint Peter defended the servant and berated the Ankou for wishing capricious death on an honest man engaged in honest labor. He wished the servant an extra measure of years. And as for the Ankou, Saint Peter struck the creature blind, putting out the light in the deathly eyes.

Whether the story is true or not, blindness hindered the Ankou very little. From dusk to the hour just before dawn, he continued to travel the roads and byways of Brittany, from Nantes to Rennes to Finistère, patiently waiting for those who ignored the curfew bells. The unwary would find themselves struck between the shoulder blades by a heavy hand, pushed face down into the dirt of the ditches, their nostrils filled with the earth that soon would be their home. Those trapped thus at dusk were lucky: They might live for another two years. But the people who met the Ankou late at night would die before the month was out.

The Ankou was a plodding workman himself, with his wide-brimmed hat, his creaking wooden death cart and his limitless, quiet patience. In this respect, he was quite different from the death harbingers to the north and east.

In Germany and Scandinavia, in Scotland and Wales and England, Death came for his victims with a cold, triumphant shout. He rode a mighty horse and led a wild troop of huntsmen across the night sky. When silvered clouds scudded past the moon's face, the troop might appear as shadows galloping on the winds, surrounded by spectral hounds. The shouts and laughter of the riders often carried to the people huddled in cottage and castle far below, and few dared venture out when the winds howled and whined. It was better not to look, for a glimpse of the huntsman of souls brought madness and death.

The tale was told in Devon, for instance, of a farmer who returned late one night from Widecombe Fair, somewhat the worse for the ale he had drunk, but able to guide his mare along the muddy lanes that led to his village. Wind raged in the trees around him, and flashes of lightning bleached the rattling branches. When rain began to fall, he pulled his hat down to protect his face and neck.

At length, he found his horse knee-deep in yelping hounds. The dogs danced im-

In the north of England lurked the shaggy dog called Skriker, a forerunner of Death.
To see it and to hear the hateful squelching of its feet was a terrible fate indeed.

patiently at his stirrups. He looked up: A black-clad huntsman stood motionless before him, astride a gleaming black horse. The huntman's own broad-brimmed hat hid his face in shadow. There were bodies—of what animals the farmer could not tell—slung across the huntsman's saddle.

The farmer noted the great lord's booty and, in his distinctly bibulous state, cackled with laughter. "Huntsman, share your spoils," said he.

The huntsman looked down at him and shrugged and laughed in his turn. He tossed a parcel at the farmer, wheeled his horse and disappeared into the night, taking his hounds with him.

With rain-slicked hands, the farmer fumbled at the parcel. The wrappings fell away, and the man started violently. The parcel held the body of his small son, blue and stiff. Yet when the farmer blinked and looked again, all he saw were his own wet hands. He kicked his mare and sped home as fast as the beast could travel. His wife awaited him, wailing. The infant boy she held in her arms was dead.

People speculated about the identity of the huntsman who rode the night skies and pierced the air with his shouts and horn blasts. In the northern lands, he was said to be Woden, god of the Norse and Teutonic tribes that had roamed the vast forests of Scandinavia and Germany. Preceded by owls and attended by ravens, the god bestrode a milk white horse; around him the fabric of his great cloak rose sail-like into the air, and his bright eyes were alert for unwary mortals.

In Wales the wild hunt's leader was identified as Gwyn ap Nudd, King of the underworld; in England the leader of the sky riders was variously said to be the ancient British King Herla, King Arthur, or Herne, a huntsman who had hanged himself from an oak in Windsor Forest and paid for the suicide by riding forever. Sometimes the huntsman was called simply Death, or the devil. As for his henchmen, that whooping, screeching, horn-blowing host, they were thought to be the tormented souls of the dead, come back to help in the harvest of victims.

The Cornish had another name—and a tale behind it—for the huntsman. They called him Dando.

Dando was a medieval priest whose parish was the pretty village of St. Germans, settled on an inlet high above the bracken-covered slate cliffs of the southern coast of the peninsula. He was hardly a model of priestly rectitude: Below his gleaming tonsure, a fat face bulged, laced with a network of veins that spoke of drink and self-indulgence. And, in fact, wine, the riotous company of the young bucks of the town, and the attentions of complaisant young women led Dando's list of earthly pleasures. He was also enamored of hunting. Many a day when he should have been tending to his priestly duties, he could be found galloping through the valleys and over the high pastures of the region, trailing a pack of hounds in search of deer, fox and any small game that dared appear.

One autumn Sunday—of all days for such a man to follow such pursuits—Dando and his merry company ranged out

To see the banshee, said the Irish, meant to foresee one's own death. This sad harbinger often appeared as a pale young woman, washing graveclothes in lonely streams.

across the countryside, thirty or forty strong. They thundered across the tiny freeholds of the neighborhood, trampling the grain and leaving in their wake a jumble of uprooted onions and turnips and a scattering of terrified sheep. The farmers who worked the little plots clenched their fists when they saw the damage, but any curses were only muttered, for people feared priestly powers in those days, even the powers of such a priest as Dando.

As the raucous company surged north toward distant Bodmin Moor, it was joined by a stranger, a tall, saturnine man mounted on a black horse. He emerged from a copse and galloped to Dando's flank. The stranger said nothing, but he easily kept pace with the priest, thrusting ahead of the pack.

The stranger rode with the hunters only a few moments, however, for the dogs were tiring in the noon heat, the horses were foam-flecked and the men red-faced. Dando, his habit hiked above his fat knees for coolness, reined in his mount and raised his hand to halt the riders.

They had stopped in the midst of an empty, rolling moor, and they clustered together. The hounds dropped to the ground to rest, and Dando bellowed for drink. But, as his servant reported, no drink was to be had. He had drunk it all.

"Well, then, if you can find none here, go to hell for it," said Dando in a fury.

The stranger who had joined them, still cool and unruffled, bowed from his saddle and proffered a golden drinking horn.

"Here is some drink from the place you mention," he said evenly. Dando, without so much as a "thank you," took the horn and drained it dry. The stranger made no remark, but he never took his eyes off the priest. At length, wiping his mouth on the greasy sleeve of his habit, Dando roundly declared that never in his life had he tasted drink so good. He roared an oath and told his men that gods must drink such nectar.

"Well, gods do not," said the stranger. "But devils do."

Dando swayed in the saddle. "If they do," said he, "then I wish I was a devil."

The stranger said nothing, but he did a curious thing. He dismounted and began to gather the rabbits and birds—the morning's catch—that had been laid on the ground by the company's servants.

"Stop that, man. None of those are yours," snarled the priest. But the stranger paid him no heed. With quick, deft gestures, he tied the animals to his saddle and mounted again. "What I have," he remarked quietly, "I hold." He watched impassively as Dando lurched to his side.

Dando tugged at the animals tied to the saddle and squinted up into the stranger's face. He spoke with the careful deliberation of the very drunk. "These are mine. I will

When nights were long and cold and dark, the Ankou rode the lanes of Brittany, searching for souls. The Bretons said the creature was Death himself, and they closed their ears against the sound of his creaking cart.

have them back from you if I must go to hell for them."

"And so you will," said the stranger. He leaned from the saddle and, with astonishing strength, lifted the priest from the ground and placed him before him. Then, holding the priest steady with an arm of iron, he spurred his horse away.

Dando's men stared open-mouthed, but his hounds gave chase at once, across the moors and through the valleys. At last they came to the banks of the River Lynher. Without hesitation, the horseman and his cargo leaped into the deep waters. Dando's hounds swam after him.

The farmers and fishermen who saw the strange scene said that Dando, the stranger and the dogs vanished into the waters in a great pillar of flame, leaving the river bubbling and steaming. The countryfolk waited for the bodies to surface, but none

ever did. Dando and his dogs were never seen alive again.

But on Sunday mornings in the months and years that followed, before the dawning sun stabbed light across the Cornish fields and the waters of the Lynher, Dando reappeared on his hunting ground—a pale, fat man with glittering eyes, mounted on a pale horse and followed by a pack of ember-eyed hounds. He terrorized the countryside around St. Germans and beyond; the priest had come to do Death's work, harvesting the souls of the living, and the sound of his pack was long feared.

Such death dealers as Dando and the Ankou and even the devil—when he rode as a huntsman of souls—generally carried out labors at a measured pace. They struck down a cottager here and a townsman there, and perhaps a prince or prelate in between. Death seemed on occasion to be

Their great horses screaming, their hellhounds howling, the riders of the Wild Hunt coursed the northern skies. A host of the dead, they sought new companions from among the living.

untimely, but it scarcely disturbed the even tenor of the world; if the number of the living was diminished by the exit of the dying, that number was also replenished by the entrance of the newly born.

There were times, though, when the balance seemed broken and the whole world dying, and in those times, Death was provided with a troop of special harbingers. Such a time began in the 14th Century.

Early in the century there were rumors of pestilence in central Asia, but people in Europe, preoccupied with the wars, bad harvests and famines that were prevalent then, paid little attention. Sometime in October of 1347, however, twelve Genoese galleys—probably bearing Asian goods channeled through the Crimea, a major stop on the silk road from the East—landed at the port of Messina on the island of Sicily. They bore crews who, the chroniclers said, had "sickness clinging to their very bones." They also bore a population of fleas that rested comfortably in bales of cloth or in the hair of that well-traveled vagabond, the black rat, *Rattus rattus*.

None of this was particularly unusual for the period, with the exception of the fleas. They were of a type known by the Egyptian-sounding name of *X. Cheopsis*, and in their stomachs they carried the plague bacillus, imported along the silk route from Asia.

The disease had three forms. There was a bubonic type, so called because of the immense boils, or buboes, that formed on the lymph nodes of the victims. This form killed within a week. The pneumonic plague, in which the bacillus infected the lungs, causing spitting of blood, killed in less than two days. Those whose blood was invaded by the third form, septicemic plague, died within an hour or two. The disease was horrible in any of these versions, with symptoms so repellent that the sufferers often became objects of disgust; it robbed their deaths of any dignity.

And it spread like wildfire. "Many died daily or nightly in the public streets," wrote the Italian poet Boccaccio. "Of many others, who died at home, the departure was hardly observed by their neighbors, until the stench of their putrefying bodies carried the tidings; and what with their corpses and the corpses of others who died on every hand, the whole place was a sepulcher."

Within days, the citizens of Messina were dying by the hundreds. The processions they conducted to ask for divine mercy were attacked, it was said, by a monstrous black dog—an ominous event indeed. Within a few months, moving along the trade routes, the plague had invaded Rome and Tuscany; by January of 1348 it had reached Marseilles, and by June it was ravaging Paris and Bavaria. Early in the following year the plague reached England and Scandinavia: It was said that a wool ship sailing from London to Norway carried—unbeknownst to the captain—one infected crew member; within a few days, all the crew were dead, and the ship drifted aimlessly until it ran aground near Bergen. The citizens, baffled by the silent ship crowded with dead men, ventured aboard and saw, too late, the black spots and empurpled faces that marked the passage of the plague.

It was a time of terror, crowded with portents of disaster. In France, stars were seen falling by the thousands; in Avignon, a column of fire rose high above the papal palace but burned nothing. The bells of St. Mark's in Venice rang, although no mortal hand had touched them. The Welsh described the plague as a "rootless phantom which has no mercy," and indeed, Death was hungry. In Scandinavia, the disease was spread, it was thought, by a pest maiden, who emerged as a flame from the mouths of the dead and flew from house to house. In Lithuania, she could be seen drifting lightly on the wind, touching

Nor crown nor coin can halt time's flight
Or stay the armies of the night.
King and villein, lad and lass,
All answer to the hourglass.

down here and there. When she alighted, she waved a red scarf into the window or door of the house she had chosen, and all who lived within soon died.

An oft-related story of the time tells of a brave farmer who waited at his window, watching the fields and the road that led to neighboring villages. At last he spied the maiden, the scarf trailing from her flesh-less hand, drifting toward his own house, which stood on the very edge of his vil-lage. The white face came closer, until he could see the burning eyes: The maiden drifted to his door, which was bolted, and then to the window where he stood. Her hand reached in toward him, bearing the scarf. He chopped the hand off with his ax, and although he and his family died, his village was saved.

According to the chroniclers, "a third of the world died." Whole villages van-ished, and birds and foxes nested in the abandoned churches. Fields lay fallow, weed-choked and brown because there was no one left to plow them. Vagabonds thronged the roads, freed from the land by the deaths of overseers and lords of the manors. Now they had no work to do, no place to live and no food to eat. Famine followed plague and war followed famine; the troubles of that sad century seemed to have no limit.

But gradually, as is the way with an epi-demic disease, the plague died down. Per-haps the plague maiden was sated. At any rate, for the next several centuries, the populations of Europe suffered no horrors commensurate with those brought by the disease in its early years.

In the bleak winter of 1665, however,

A miser thought to keep his gold
As shield against the coming cold.
But what cared Death for mortal gains?
He smiled upon the miser's pains.

For most of the centuries of the Middle Ages, bubonic plague periodically swept through
the European countryside. Thousands of people fell before the Reaper's swinging
scythe, and whole villages disappeared from the face of the earth.

and from the mouth of a ghost, came an eerie foretelling, an indication that the scythe of the plague was once more honed and ready to sweep across the land.

It happened in January, in the parish of South Petherwin in Cornwall. The curate there, John Rudall, recorded it in his diary. One afternoon, Rudall wrote, he was summoned to Botathen House, the seat of one of his parishoners, a man named Bligh. Rudall found Bligh in some distress, asking for a private talk. Together the men walked along the paths of a winter-bare garden, and Bligh told a strange tale indeed.

His small son, he said, was haunted. Each morning, when the boy crossed a meadow near the house on his way to school, he was approached by an apparition. The image of a white-faced young woman came toward him, not walking on the grass but drifting in the air a few inches above it. Its eyes were fixed on the boy, and something about its demeanor frightened him so much that he was reluctant to approach the field.

Bligh might have dismissed this story as an imaginative schoolboy's invention except for one detail: The boy recognized the apparition. It was, he claimed, a young woman named Dorothy Dinglet, who had long been a friend of the Bligh family and who had died three years before.

Bligh finished his account, and Rudall regarded him in thoughtful silence. Then the curate, a practical man, said that they should go to the meadow and see for themselves whether the dead indeed walked.

Accordingly, at dawn the next day, the two men went to the spot. The boy walked between them, clutching their hands in fear, and his spaniel trotted alongside. At first, they saw nothing more than the brown, frost-rimmed stubble of winter grass. But presently, in a far corner of the field, they discerned a faint shape that grew firmer in outline as it approached them. It was truly Dorothy Dinglet, quivering and shifting in the morning light. Her hair, as Rudall later wrote, was so soft that it seemed to melt away as he looked.

The ghost gazed piteously at the curate. He asked it to speak and prove itself no fiend. After a moment, a soft voice said, "Before next Yuletide, a fearful pestilence will lay waste the land, and myriads of souls will be loosened from their flesh." The men shuddered. At their feet, the boy's spaniel whined once and then was silent.

Using the powers of his office, Rudall eventually gave the ghost rest *(page 125)*, but he remembered the words she had spoken. They were to prove true, and all too soon. In June of that year, heat descended on the British Isles. Day after day the sun blazed unrelentingly down on the parched fields and pastures. The Thames River was sluggish and low, and its stench drifted throughout London, a city cloaked in a dull, yellow haze.

Then the plague maiden and her kind struck. All over the city, blood red crosses

Her hour had come; his mother smiled
And sighed beside her infant child.
But he, too, answered to the curse
And found himself an older nurse.

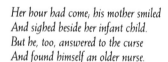

Out in the shadows, endlessly washing ill-gotten gains, the ghost of the
squire of Swinsty Hall did penance for robberies of victims of the plague.

appeared on the doors of the houses of the victims, with the pitiful inscription, "Lord have mercy upon us," scribbled beneath. All over the city, bloated and blackened bodies lay unclaimed in the narrow streets. There was no one left to bury them except the drivers of death carts; they gathered up the corpses and dumped them into plague pits – mass graves dug on the outskirts of London.

During the summer, the disease spread into the countryside, decimating towns and villages alike. It raged unchecked until the winter cold killed the fleas that harbored the bacillus. By that time, seventy-five thousand people had died. Then the plague abated, having made its last horrific flourish in England. There would be smaller epidemics, but none to match the nightmare of 1665.

That nightmare would be long remembered – vividly reenacted in visitations by those who had died during the plague year. One such spectral visitor regularly appeared near the village of Vernham Dean in Hampshire. Through Vernham Dean runs a Roman road called Chute Causeway. Its course takes it along the crest of a hill not far from the village. For centuries, on nights when the moon gleamed through banks of clouds and owls hooted mournfully in the trees nearby, the silhouette of a man could be seen on the causeway. Bent beneath a huge sack, dragging wooden buckets, the figure toiled alone, its legs moving slowly up the hillside. But it never advanced; it never reached the summit.

That, folk whispered generation after generation, was the shade of a clergyman who had deserted his flock. He was a good man, it was said, and in the year of the plague he had urged the people of Vernham Dean to abandon their homes in the village and isolate themselves in a camp on top of the hill, where the air was fresh and free from contagion. The pastor himself would remain behind, to keep an eye on their belongings, he said. And he promised to carry food and drink to them every day.

The villagers agreed and retreated to the hilltop, but the plague was already among them, and the moans of the dying soon eddied down to the village. They died, every one – died without succor and

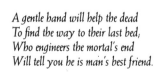

A gentle hand will help the dead
To find the way to their last bed;
Who engineers the mortal's end
Will tell you he is man's best friend.

without even the ease of food and drink promised them by their pastor. Frightened for his life, he never appeared to them. And thus he was doomed to haunt the hillside forever, human without humanity, darker than the surrounding darkness, staggering beneath a burden of guilt that would never find redemption.

Far from Hampshire, in the vale of Washburn in the north of England, another plague scene was played out night after moonlit night. By a little stream that ran through the vale, a hunched figure could be seen scrubbing and rinsing, rinsing and scrubbing. It was trying to cleanse a pile of coins, but all the waters in England were not enough to remove the stain from that money.

The coins had come from plague-ridden London in the endless summer of death, when rats gnawed the corpses of victims and human vermin ruled the streets. One of that crew was a wretch named Robinson, who scuttled from house to house, relieving the dead and the helpless dying of their money and their valuables.

Robinson was second to none in the depths to which he would stoop. Not even the coins placed upon the eyes of the unseeing dead to keep them closed were safe from his grasp.

His activities were ended by a wisp of smoke that arose one September night from the neighborhood of Pudding Lane, near London Bridge. Within moments, flames driven by an east wind spread unchecked across the city. The Great Fire of London, a disaster mitigated only by the fact that it heralded winter and an end to the plague, had begun.

Of the thousands who fled the city, one was Robinson, who hastily loaded his plunder onto a wagon and fled alone to the north, to the village where he had been born. He was unwelcome: The people of his village feared that he brought the plague with him. Driven from his village, he lived in a barn and occupied his waking hours with washing his stolen coins in a stream, hoping to cleanse them of any trace of pestilence.

Eventually, Robinson built a great country house called Swinsty Hall, and there he lived out his days in luxury. But after his natural death in a warm, soft bed, he was called to reckoning. The house he had built with the money of the dead fell into other hands. And at the stream not far from the house, Robinson forever paid his penance.

The squire of Swinsty Hall and the pastor of Vernham Dean were but two examples of a ghostly throng that memorialized the miseries of 1665. The events that kept them chained to the world of the living were extraordinary, but their basic motives for haunting were not unusual. Like many ghosts, these two creatures did nothing but harmlessly repeat their crimes for centuries, making a kind of lantern-slide show of iniquity.

More to be feared were the envious or vengeful spirits left behind by the scythe of Death. Their prey was the living, and their powers of terrorizing were great. Their hauntings, as will be told, came to be more feared than the coming of the Reaper himself.

Song of the Sorrowing Harp

On the east coast of Scotland, in a castle hard by the North Sea, lived a lord who had two daughters, the elder one dark, the younger fair. As sometimes happens, the maidens were rivals—although the younger sister did not know it and the elder would not admit it—and something occurred between them that caused a ghost to speak.

A young lord came courting. Quite properly, he paid formal addresses to the elder sister, but his eyes always strayed to the younger. He rode by her at the hunt; he danced with her in the hall. And all the while, the dark gaze of the elder sister followed him. She made no complaint, biding her time.

Early one morning, the elder maiden asked her sister to walk by the seashore. As they strolled, the fair sister spoke guilessly about the dashing visitor. The elder said little, but at a place where the waves beat against massive rocks, she acted. With a swift blow, she knocked her sister off balance and into the foaming sea.

The waves closed over the fair maiden's head and clawed at her hair with icy fingers. She rose gasping to the surface and screamed to her sister, but there was no response. She heard only the roaring of the waters and the sharp cries of gulls as they wheeled in the sky above. The dark sister stood on the shore rocks, motionless as a carved statue. With a steady, unperturbed gaze, she watched her sister's hopeless struggle. The young maiden sank, rose again for a moment and cried out pitifully, then sank again beneath the surging skirts of foam.

The dark one kept her vigil there for a time, observing the violence of the waves with satisfaction. Then she ran home to her father's hall and, weeping, told a false tale, saying how her sister had slipped on the rocks and drowned. The people searched the shore for her, but they could not find her body. They made great mourning in the months that followed. Afterward, the young lord, bereft of the fair sister, sought consolation with the dark, and this was gladly given.

But the fair sister's body, drawn by wind and tide and cradled in the killing waves, drifted along the Scottish shore and into a calm loch, far from her father's lands. A miller at the loch's edge spied the golden hair stirring beneath the surface and gently pulled the body from the water.

It happened that a wandering minstrel—a harper famed throughout Scotland—was staying with the miller. He helped the man to give her burial, and moved by her

beauty, he cut three strands of the golden hair and strung them into his harp.

Eventually the harper took leave of the miller and went on his way, traveling from castle to castle to sing before the lords of the land. In the months that followed, the harp played for the minstrel with a tenderness that brought tears to the eyes of its listeners, and the harper grew to cherish the golden strings.

At length he came to the stronghold of the maiden's father, although he did not know it for what it was. The minstrel was welcomed and feasted, as was the custom then. In the evening, when the fires were lit and the flames cast flickering shadows in the hall, the man drew out his harp and set it before him, making ready to sing. The dark sister settled on a bench to listen, flanked by her father and by the young lord she loved.

But before the harper could touch them, the golden strings shimmered in the firelight; they trembled of their own accord. A sweet familiar voice eddied around the company, and when the dark sister heard the words it sang, her face grew pale and tight. Her fate had come upon her, and well she knew it.

"Farewell to the lord my father," sang the harp softly. "Farewell to my lady mother."

The harp paused, and the company watched it in horrified silence. Then the strings spoke once more, loud and wailing this time.

"And woe to my sister, who murdered me."

Chapter Two

Invasions by the Angry Dead

Several centuries ago, something haunted a small fishing village huddled among the rockfalls fringing a Norwegian fjord. For five long years, something wandered near the houses and wailed on the wind. A fisherman in the village was the first to discover what it was.

This is how he learned. He lay one night among his family in their hut of roughly chinked logs, and on that night, although the wind mumbled around the walls and rattled at the latch, no crying voice was heard and no footsteps pattered outside. For the first time in years, the only noises were natural ones, and the fisherman slept soundly.

In the small hours, however, he was roused by the goats that shared the family's hut. They had begun to shuffle uneasily in the straw. He looked around with the heightened alertness of the suddenly awakened. But nothing seemed amiss. The air was close with the fetor of animals and the breath of the sleeping children, nestled together for warmth. Beside him, his wife lay deep in dreams.

Then he saw what had disturbed the goats. A patch of moonlight fell on the back of the door, and in its light the fisherman discerned a thin thread of smoke uncoiling from the keyhole. The merest wisp of vapor, it sank lazily toward the floor, vanishing in the gloom. The man's eyes strained to follow it and caught, near the base of the door, a glimmer uncannily like bare skin.

He watched transfixed as the faint luminosity resolved itself into human—or near-human—form. Crawling from the darkness, its skin blue with cold, its ribs starting from a withered torso and its wide eyes fastened on his own, was an apparition of his own child, an infant boy who had died five years before. The ghost approached across the straw-strewn floor in silence. Jolted into action at last, the man shook his wife awake.

She gave a whimper of recognition as the infant crept across her legs and belly. The man snatched at the small figure, thinking to pull it away, but his hands closed on a substance as cold, hard and inexorable as glacial ice. His wife gasped for breath as the weight of the ghost crushed her chest. The little arms reached for her face. Tiny hands churned for an instant in the mother's eye sockets, and the next moment, the apparition was gone. The woman's whimper rose to a scream, and blood welled where her eyes had been. She was blind. The following night, the wailing and the pattering in the lanes around the village began again – and would continue for many years.

The vengeful infant ghost that maimed its mother was known as an *utburd*, from the old Norse word for "child carried outside." It had been born sickly into a family that already had too many mouths to feed, and it had been exposed: The fisherman and his wife had scratched a shallow grave in the snowbound wilds outside their hamlet and left the child alone there to die and stiffen in the stinging cold. Death soon released the child's spirit from the little body. Later that same day, the fisherman covered the grave.

He and his wife had felt no remorse. In the harsh lands of the North, it was common practice to expose infants in times of want, or when the mother was unwed or when the child was sickly or malformed. Justified though the act seemed to the adults who performed it, the ghosts that sprang from the tiny corpses burned for revenge. And, as if in compensation for the infants' helplessness during their few days of life, *utburds* were formidable ghosts, gathering strength in the years after their deaths until they could make their vengeance complete.

Ordinarily, an *utburd* was invisible, although its doleful cries often rang out across the stony wastes near the little grave it rose from. But a sharp-eyed traveler who heard the cries might glimpse a snowy-plumed owl, skimming low over the distant tundra, or a black dog, waist-high and shaggy, silhouetted on a far ridgetop. Or, beneath a nearby shrub, he might even discern for a moment the phantom of the murdered infant itself, its tiny fists clenched in pain or rage. People said that, in any of its guises, an *utburd* could swell to the height of a cowshed. When it returned to its birthplace to seek out its mother, however, it dwindled to a curl of smoke, able to slip into a dwelling and take shape again with all its hideous strength intact, ready to savor its revenge.

But an *utburd's* rage endured long after its mother was in her grave, and it continued to claim victims – usually solitary wayfarers. An encounter with an *utburd* was intimate and terrifying. Thunderous footfalls, resounding like boulders dropped from a great height, signaled the approach of the ghost. Most travelers knew better than to look back, for a glimpse of the pursuing *utburd* – if it was visible – could paralyze a mortal. When the traveler broke into a run, the massive footsteps, merging into an unbroken roar, kept pace easily. And when the victim tired, the *utburd's* cold clasp would tighten about his chest, dragging him to the ground with an irresistible weight.

Water and iron, substances inimical to ghosts, could save a mortal pursued by an *utburd*. If the traveler splashed into a stream or unsheathed a pocket knife in time, he would find himself alone and unscathed in the silent wilderness. More often, though, another wayfarer would happen upon the body days or weeks later, its bones crushed and its flesh shredded by supernatural strength and fury.

Few spirits matched the *utburd* in brutality, but in other respects, its activities were representative of a certain kind of ghost. A multitude of spirits bedeviled the living, variously motivated by vengeance, envy and a mindless quest for attention. They inflicted suffering of every kind: Some, like the *utburd*, threatened physical attack; others energetically disrupted the routines of mortal existence; still others, although evanescent and harmless, chilled their beholders through the sheer horror of their aspect.

The physical prowess of the *utburd* was not unique. Although the words "ghost" and "spirit" both imply a phenomenon as tenuous as the human soul, some ghosts retained the bulk and strength of their mortal bodies. From the grave mounds of Scandinavia came ghosts as substantial and powerful as the brawny warriors buried there. These were risen corpses, blackened and swollen from their entombment in the chill earth. The sign heralding the emergence of such a barrow-wight — so called from the barrow, or grave mound, that it infested — was the discovery of the body of a herdsman or wanderer, horribly brutalized during the hours of darkness.

Such ghosts were sustained, as was the *utburd*, by malevolence. Most had been disputatious and aggressive in their lifetimes, and release from the confinement of the ordered world of the living had given free rein to their chaotic natures. They were strengthened by death.

Outside Scandinavia, most ghosts of this type stopped short of actual attacks on the living. Simply spreading panic and dread was enough, it seemed. Such was the case with the venomous spirit of a certain Lord Lonsdale, bane of the Westmorland countryside in England two centuries ago.

It surprised no one that this rapacious aristocrat, given to quarreling with neighbors and flogging peasants who could not meet his criminal exactions of grain and livestock, did not submit quietly to the tomb. As the vicar knelt praying at the coffin, the body sat up abruptly. One massive shoulder caught the clergyman in the chest and sent him sprawling, gasping more in fright than in pain. The corpse's eyes opened and bulged, as if it had startled itself; then its lids closed and it settled back onto the satin pillows. Once sealed in the coffin, though, the corpse was quiet, and its burial was seemly.

But that was by no means the last of the Bad Lord, as he had long been known. The unruly corpse spawned a rambunctious ghost whose heavy footsteps and destructive rage made a bedlam of the upper floors of Lowther Hall, the Bad Lord's erstwhile residence. Those few of Lonsdale's kinsmen who dared remain on the premises cowered in chambers downstairs, cringing at the ghost's hoarse bellows and the sound of splintering furniture. Occasionally the ghost strode into view at the head of the great stairway, its face an even more choleric red than it had been in life. It shook its fist at the fearful mortals gathered at the foot of the stairs, then continued its solitary rampage.

The Bad Lord did not confine his displays of spleen to Lowther Hall. On nights when the house fell ominously silent, servants scattered through the neighborhood

Flames that yielded endless cold

Dancing by night over bogs, brakes and water meadows, the flamelike luminance called *ignis fatuus*, or "foolish fire," once was common throughout northern Europe. Although the learned would claim that the flames were caused by marsh gases, countryfolk knew better, and tales of mishaps made them wary.

The strange light was given myriad names – "will-o'-the-wisp," "jack-o'-lantern," "fox fire," "elf light." In Wales, the flames were called "corpse candles" and appeared just at the level of a raised human hand when a ghost walked invisible; they were thought to presage the death of those who saw them. Germans said the lights were the ghosts of those who had stolen land. For Finns, such a light was a *liekkiö*, or "flaming one," and was believed to be the ghost of a child who had been buried in the forest.

In any case, the dancing flames were dangers to the living. Wayfarers who mistook them for the lights of a far-off shelter sometimes strayed into thickets where the ground grew shifty and sucked them down into the depths of bogs. Those who followed ghost lights, people said, were led to join the company of Death.

to warn the farmfolk not to leave their cottages. For along the highroads, swift as the night wind, clattered a phantom—a black coach that terrorized wayfarers, panicking horses and running other carriages into the ditches. Torches blazed at its corners, shedding a lurid glare into the darkness, and on the driver's bench, as menacing and highhanded as ever, sat the Bad Lord Lonsdale. This went on for months. Finally a wise neighbor, skilled in the art of stilling spirits, marshaled his powers against the apparition, and Lowther Hall and the surrounding district were fully in the possession of the living once again.

Lord Lonsdale's was a blustery spirit, a marauder in the mortal world. But at least people knew what the ghost was—an expression of the personality of a villain they all recognized. Another sort of ghost—a poltergeist—behaved in much the same violent manner as Lord Lonsdale's spirit but was doubly frightening because no one could tell where it hailed from, and no one knew how to dismiss it.

Poltergeists—the word is German for "racketing spirits"—were a mass of unknowns. Their physical disruptions of households served no discernible purpose of revenge; neither did they express the malevolence of a departed neighbor or kinsman, active even in death. Most poltergeists, in fact, could not be identified as spirits of the dead. If they did spring from the realm of death, they were anonymous envoys: They were bodiless and rarely visible, and their utterances almost never took shape as speech.

The details that recur in accounts of poltergeist hauntings only deepen the enigma. Poltergeists chose as targets the world's innocents: They had a predilection for the families of clergymen, and within those families they often singled out as the focus of their activities a young girl—a daughter or a maidservant. Their tactics—thumping, howling, the hurling of objects and creation of bad smells—seemed calculated to attract maximum attention with minimum physical harm.

That is not to say that a poltergeist infestation was a trifling inconvenience. Poltergeists had limitless stamina. Even gentle poltergeist mischief—slammed doors, upended cream pots, whiffs of sulfur—grew unendurable when the poltergeist sustained it day and night for weeks or months. And often such mild mischief was punctuated by bursts of destructive energy difficult to credit from an incorporeal and invisible spirit. Yet a few families, especially tolerant or humorous, grew inured to their spirit guests, after the initial terror of the haunting faded. In time, a poltergeist might even come to be accepted as a slightly eccentric member of the family. This happened in Epworth, an old English market town in Lincolnshire.

The poltergeist haunting of Epworth Rectory began with a vigorous overture of disturbances. The family of the Reverend Samuel Wesley was large—he had

Ghost children who called from the dark

Among the various sorts of ghosts that confronted travelers, few were as piteous as the *navky*, haunters of Slavic lands. They were the spirits of children who had died unbaptized or at their mother's hands. Most often they appeared in the shapes of infants or young girls, rocking in tree branches and wailing and crying in the night. Some begged for baptism from passersby. Some—thirsting for revenge against the living, who had let them die nameless—lured unwitting travelers into perilous places. But they were not always human in form: In Yugoslavia, it was said, the *navky* took the shapes of great black birds, which cried in a manner that chilled the soul.

ten children – and the ghost manifested itself to one after another of the members, until its activity could no longer be dismissed as a prank or a case of an overheated imagination. But the unfortunate servants were the first to witness it.

The ghost announced itself late one December evening in 1716 with a knock on the door, followed by a low groan. A manservant and maidservant, sitting up late, opened the door to find only an empty doorsill, with black night behind. They looked into the gloom, listened intently for a while and finally concluded that the disturbances were someone's notion of a joke. But when they returned to their tea

Invisible demons of domestic disorder, the ghosts called poltergeists had boundless energy
and a gift for the unpleasant surprise. Their pleasure was chaos, and when
they went haunting, no object in a house was safe from destruction.

and small talk, the knock came again, hard enough to rattle the door in its frame. Again the servants peered out the door into emptiness. Edgy now, wary even of the shadows that danced across the candlelight, they bade each other good night.

As the manservant climbed the back stairs to the garret, he heard a busy whir-ring and was startled to see his shadow etched on the wall next to the stairs by an unfamiliar brightness. He crouched to look between the balusters into the kitch-en, inexplicably ablaze with light. The hearth was bare and cold, the pots and caldrons empty and scrubbed, and the scullery maids in bed. But on its oaken

table, the iron hand mill used for grinding grain was noisily in motion. Its crank whirled briskly, yet the machine ground nothing, and the force that drove it was nowhere to be seen. The servant blinked, hoping to erase the image and restore propriety to his surroundings. But the mill spun apace, and the servant hurried to bed, determined to ignore the manic whir.

Just as he dozed off, he was jolted into wakefulness by another unaccountable sound: the gobbling of a turkey, close by his pillow. He clawed at the darkness and felt nothing. Then, from the foot of his bed, came the clatter and thud of a man tripping over boots. The servant sat bolt upright. With cautious fingers, he groped for his boots. They stood where he had left them, neatly beneath the bed, well out of range of any mortal tread.

The servants' anxious morning reports at first met with incredulity from the masters and scorn from the other servants. But during the days that followed, doubt gave way to appalled certainty.

The ghost's activities reflected no pattern, pursuit or character—nothing but a childlike quest for notice. The poltergeist might sweep into a room with the sound of rustling silk petticoats, weave gracefully around the furniture and whisk out again, gently closing the door behind it. On another occasion, it might climb the stairs with the tread of an ironshod ogre, rattling windowpanes all around the house and lofting puffs of dust from forgotten corners. At one instant, the spirit might be heard knocking on doors and windows

and shaking latches in an idiot frenzy; the next, having passed stealthily and silently into the room through a locked door or a shuttered window, it would hover in midair and utter a deep and inhuman groan—a "dead hollow note," in Wesley's words—that overwhelmed any other sound in the room.

From time to time, the Epworth ghost, wearying of mere noise and disorder, tantalized and unnerved the family with fleeting apparitions. Three weeks after the haunting began, Mrs. Wesley—her curiosity overcoming fear—pushed open the door to the empty nursery in which the ghost's customary racket resounded. At once the room was silent, but Mrs. Wesley sensed a presence. She gazed around her, then, on a whim, bent to look under the bed. There was a rattle of claws, and something swift and shadowy scuttled past the terrified woman and out the door—no mouse or rat, she later recalled, but something "like a badger." When she had collected herself, she ordered the servants to search the house, but no creature of any description was found.

Later during the Wesley family's siege, another shadowy creature emerged from a storage nook in the kitchen. When a servant, sitting up late by the fire, turned to get a clear view of the shape, it spun around on the flagstones five times—looking in its blur like a small rabbit—then darted back into the nook. And when the man crept close, the niche was empty. Whether

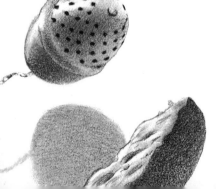

such uncanny animal apparitions embodied the poltergeist, or whether they were visual pranks conjured by the poltergeist to vex its human hosts, none who experienced the Epworth spirit could say.

In the end, the Wesleys accepted their visitor with resigned good humor. They dubbed it Old Jeffrey, after a former tenant of the rectory, said to have died there — although they had no reason to believe that their tormentor was the dead man's spirit. The children, better able to adapt to its senseless disruptions than the adults, eventually began to treat the ghost as a kind of rambunctious pet: They amused themselves by dashing toward the current focus of uproar, hoping to reach it before the poltergeist moved on to another part of the house. Only the Wesley mastiff — like most animals more sensitive than humans to the supernatural — never grew accustomed to the ghost. At each riotous outburst, the beast's tail drooped and the dog retired, whimpering and trembling, to a corner of the parlor.

Perhaps it was the Wesley family's equanimity that at last freed them from their bumptious visitor; perhaps the ghost grew restive when it could no longer terrorize. Two months after the phenomenon began, the Wesley family gathered as usual for morning prayers. Two knocks at the head of the stairs answered the murmured "amen" — blows so gentle that the family, accustomed to uproar, hardly noticed them. After that, all was silence.

That was the last of the Wesley poltergeist. It left forever, the cause of its retreat as much a puzzle as its advent had been. Like most poltergeists, it had demonstrated complete control over objects and a great capacity to menace with sound and with illusion. These were its only physical manifestations, and again, this was usual among poltergeists: They rarely appeared in any readily identifiable form.

The chilling exception was a nocturnal display produced toward the end of the 19th Century, when a Russian family was assaulted by a poltergeist with much the same tenacity as the ghost at the Epworth Rectory. It rocked the house with thumpings and the heavy, frenzied footsteps of a folk dancer. Later it added fire to its effects, setting ablaze the lady of the house and releasing a swarm of burning orbs that chased one another across the veranda.

All through the invasion, the family had refused to abandon the house. But then the poltergeist resorted to a new level of illusion. One morning, dozing in bed after his wife had risen, the master of the house heard a rustling in the bedclothes beside him. Expecting to find his wife, he turned toward the noise. A foot or so from his face, a tiny pink hand, disembodied but smooth-skinned even where it should have joined a wrist, toyed with the covers. Whimsically, it plucked at the coverlet, drawing it up into hills and ridges and smoothing it flat again. The man watched, paralyzed, dreading that the thing would touch him and he would have to endure the scampering pinches of the pink fingers on his face.

It danced to the edge of his pillow and paused, drumming lightly on the linen. He could bear the tension no longer. Panicked as he had not been by weeks of noise and unearthly happenings, he slipped out of the bed, fled downstairs and, still in his nightshirt, ushered his wife out of the house. The couple never returned, and the poltergeist did not follow them. After all, it had the house to itself.

In their assaults on the living, some spirits worked in quiet ways, relying on persistence rather than violence or chaotic energy. A haunting of this kind took place in the late 18th Century on a British slaver, bound from Liverpool to the Slave Coast of Africa to load its hapless cargo. Within a few days of leaving port, the ship was racked with discord. The captain was harsh and quick-tempered, and in his general displeasure with the crew he nursed a particular hate for a man named Bill Jones—aging, stout and slow at his tasks, but uncowed when the captain bellowed and cursed at him.

One day as the wind freshened, the captain gave orders to shorten sail. As always, Jones puffed and sweated with effort but worked at half the speed of his comrades. The captain took relish in berating him mercilessly when he returned to the deck—although most captains rarely spoke at all to the humbler crew members. The old sailor bore it for a time. At length, however, he turned on the captain, his face twisted with fury, and loosed a barrage of insolence that left the crew dumbstruck.

The captain, pale with rage, stumbled down the companionway that led to his cabin and returned with a blunderbuss. Its muzzle was packed with nails and iron slugs, and the captain took deadly aim and fired. Jones was flung backward, his chest horribly torn. He sighed as his life slipped away, but when he saw the captain regarding him contemptuously, his gaze grew fierce. "Sir," he gasped, "you have done for me now, but I will never leave you." He died without saying another word.

Fearful of mortal authorities, the captain swore his crew to silence, but he had more to contend with than the collective memory of the sailors. For the murdered man's spirit walked. Unheard and for the most part unseen, it joined the crew in the daily round of duty, a stolid toiler whose progress was marked by casks that seemed to shift themselves and a solitary rag that mopped the decks and polished the fittings without the urging of mortal hands.

Only up on the yards did the phantom show itself to the crew. A man busy wrestling with the canvas would feel the spar shudder beneath him; he would glance to one side and gaze aghast at the bulky figure of Jones sitting beside him, as deliberate and painstaking in death as ever he had been in life. But when the man blinked, or turned away to gesture to a sailor on deck, the apparition would vanish—although the telltale trembling continued.

The captain alone never ceased to see the ghost. He confessed to the first mate that the spirit hovered by him every minute of the day. Even at night, when he tossed and woke, he found himself fixed by the ghost's steady gaze. He beseeched the mate to take (continued on page 56)

THE WIFE'S REVENGE

In Japan there once lived a man who, by his vicious actions, made his wife into a ghost. The man's name was Iemon, his wife's was O'Iwa, and his motive was that he desired another woman. O'Iwa, barely risen from childbed, was given poison, which caused her hair to fall out in bloody handfuls, her eyes to start from their sockets and her pretty mouth to blacken. All through this ordeal, Iemon sneered; then he thrust her from him. In despair, she killed herself and her infant.

Iemon felt no remorse. Now he was free to do as he wished – or so he thought. He soon found that his deed had a terrifying price. With a ghoul's fury, O'Iwa appeared to him everywhere. If he sought peace in a teahouse, the lanterns, gaily painted in human likeness, assumed the staring eyes of O'Iwa and mouthed curses at him. If he walked in a garden, he would find her there, wailing over

her infant. Her bitter
accusations ceaselessly
sounded in his ears.

Defiant, Iemon mar-
ried his paramour,
thinking that the ghost
might realize the futil-
ity of further haunting.
But when he lifted his
lover's bridal veil after
the wedding, the face
looking back at him
was O'Iwa's. Howling,
he drew his sword and
beheaded the specter.
And then Iemon dis-
covered O'Iwa's final
vengeance: He had
murdered his bride,
not the ghost.

command of the ship while he fended off his spectral tormentor.

But the captain's sufferings dragged on, and his figure grew gaunt and his eyes bright with fever. By day he paced the decks, seemingly alone. His glance, however, flickered from side to side, and he rarely raised it to eye level, for there were eyes he did not care to meet. Sleep became impossible, and he spent his nights sitting up, groaning softly from time to time.

At last the captain could stand no more. One day the mate, giving orders from the afterdeck, heard a splash. He rushed to the taffrail to see the face of the captain, a scrap of white on the dark water receding in the ship's wake. The captain flickered in and out of view behind the wave crests, slipping bit by bit to an easeful death. Suddenly, however, he began to thrash. He half-rose from the water, and even at that distance, the mate discerned his terror. "He is with me even now!" came the hoarse cry over the hiss of the foam. Then the captain vanished beneath the waves, and with him went the ghost of Bill Jones — it was never again encountered on board.

The slaver's captain was undone by the relentless eyes of a ghost that hounded him day and night but never tried to injure him. And the same dogged quality is found in the hauntings of a kind of spirit that plagued not individuals but entire families, generation after generation, never posing a physical threat but always looming formidably in their victims' lives.

These spirits were the so-called screaming skulls, pestilential presences in many English country houses. To look at, they were no different from any charnel-house relicts, and they could be hefted and tossed in a grisly game of catch. But, as befitted former vessels of human intelligence, such skulls had inflexible will.

Screaming skulls were usually quiescent, since the families they afflicted quickly learned to respect their wishes — chiefly that they be undisturbed within their chosen home. While this demand was not especially onerous, the very presence of the skulls took a spiritual toll.

Often the craving of a skull to repose forever within a certain habitation reflected the dying desire of the skull's mortal owner. Such was the case at Burton Agnes Hall in Yorkshire. There, during the reign of Elizabeth I, lived a young lady named Anne Griffith, who dearly loved the hall — and then she died. On her deathbed, she exacted from her sisters a promise to sever her head from her corpse and keep it in the manor house permanently. Believing she was delirious, her sisters ignored her macabre wish, and her body was placed complete in the family vault.

But her kin had little time for quiet grief. Several days after the interment, the family awoke in terror as a ghoulish gibbering that seemed to mingle grief and mirth rang from every corner of the dark house. Stalwart young men prowled the corridors in their nightshirts, with daggers drawn, yet the source of the racket eluded them. Night after night the disturbances continued, the shrieks sometimes fading into the heavy groans of the dying, until at last the sisters decided to seek the advice of the local vicar. He reminded them of their promise to the dying girl and suggested that they open the tomb. And when the flowers so recently strewn for the burial were swept aside and torch-bearing kin descended into the vault's fetid air, the vicar's advice proved sound. For the corpse reflected Anne Griffith's dying wish: The body was not decayed, the bright dome of the cranium was bare of flesh, and mysteriously severed from the body. The head rested upright on its grinning chops, shadows dancing in its empty orbits.

The kinsmen's course was clear: They followed Anne's wish to the letter. The skull was taken to the house and placed as a ghoulish centerpiece on the table in the salon, and Burton Agnes Hall was quiet that night and every night for many years.

Later generations speculated that time might have moderated the skull's desire to retain a place of honor in the hall, but Anne Griffith's spirit vividly demonstrated the strength of its attachment. A scullery maid was the cause of the episode. Watching a cart laden with cabbages creak along the lane that wound near a kitchen window, she decided to rid the hall of its ugly guardian. She ran to the salon, snatched the skull and tossed it out the kitchen window at the cart, where it wedged among the cabbages. Instantly the driver began to curse, for his cart had halted, as if mired in mud. The old nag strained under his lashing, but the dray would not budge.

Drawn to the scene by the commotion, the master of the house ordered the maid to return the skull to the salon, but she could not bring herself to touch it. At last a young man of the family hurried outside and plucked the skull from the cabbages. The cart shot forward, tumbling the driver off his bench and redoubling his curses.

The young man gingerly returned the skull to its place. And there it stayed, regarded with renewed awe by the occupants of the hall, until another family succeeded to the premises. One evening, scornful of what seemed a worn-out superstition, they ordered the relict buried in the garden. But as a servant tamped down the earth over the skull, the shrieks heard centuries before, and vividly recorded in the tales told by the countryfolk, sounded once again in the corridors. All night the terrified family vainly sought the source of the ghoulish chorus, and worse awaited them in the morning. Their horses had gone lame, and a late frost had blackened the garden.

Without leave from his masters, an old servant borrowed a spade from one of the gardeners and dug up the skull. He shook the clods from it, cleaned the mud from its eye sockets and returned it to the hall. Peace returned. Once again the skull had bent mortals to its implacable will.

A few screaming skulls possessed a power that added immeasurably to their terror: a capacity to move from place to place — chillingly at odds with their stony, inert character. Not satisfied to reside in a chosen niche, such skulls pursued their victims, confronting hapless mortals at moments of vulnerability. These diligent haunters often had motives more urgent than a dying wish to remain at home; in one case, in the north of England, a pair of appallingly active skulls haunted a country house for reasons of revenge.

The skulls were those of a farm couple, hanged on charges trumped up by a landowner who coveted their garden plot. In life, the couple had been meek, but after their wrongful execution, their skulls set about hounding the landowner and his family with diabolical energy, screaming without provocation, bowling down the carpet into the great hall in the midst of banquets and springing onto the stairs to bar the way of family members. In the end, the torment ruined the proud family. Generation followed generation, each more spiritless than the one before, until the last heir died childless and penniless, and the line was extinguished.

Fearsome as a screaming skull's outbursts could be, its horror persisted even when it was silent. Its quiet presence, grinning and hollow-eyed, drained joy from the lives of its mortal housemates. In that respect, a screaming skull resembled the many other spirits that did not attack or threaten or pursue the living but merely flickered into view and then faded.

Such spirits could torment mortal sensibilities every bit as cruelly as more vigorous or persistent revenants. Often, the horror was rooted in the beholder's conscience or memory. An apparition could signify a loved one's death or the imminent death of the viewer himself; a ghost could confront a murderer with the evidence of his crime or return from the land

of death to reproach a heartless lover. Other specters, not linked to those who beheld them, evoked terror because their appearance was inherently horrible, bearing the grisly marks of a violent death.

Thus, with five streaming wounds on its face and head, walked the phantom of Anne Walker, murdered near Durham in England with a pickax by hirelings of a kinsman with whom she had had an incestuous relationship. Thus the legs and body of a noblewoman separately haunted the Highlands stronghold where her husband had killed her, then sawed the body in two and stuffed the pieces in a chest to hide his crime. And thus, a hideous emblem of a barbarous death, roamed the Legless Smuggler of Happisburgh, on England's Norfolk coast.

Summer dies early in that region. As the nights lengthen, tattered clouds scud across the moon and gray banks of fog roll in from the North Sea, bringing a chill to flesh and spirit. Beneath the mist, the baying of dogs falls to a whimper, and hares huddle in their burrows. Even the placid sheep grow restless, and farmers return quickly to their villages at day's end.

It was on such a night almost three centuries ago that several farmers, nearing the hamlet of Happisburgh, sensed and then saw what seemed to be an emissary of hell. From the direction of the Cart Gap, a cleft in the chalky cliffs that stand against the hammering sea, emerged the figure of a man — or part of one, for it was legless and, at first glance, headless as well.

Slowly the torso floated past, bearing in its arms a long, large bundle. Rolling from side to side in the manner of one accustomed to walking a ship's deck, it was clad in the skirted garment then worn by seafaring men, and it carried a pistol thrust into a broad leather belt with a brass buckle. As the grotesque figure moved down the road through Happisburgh, the terrified farmers saw that its head was, in fact, lolling upside down between its shoulder blades, a long pigtail trailing on the ground, its eyes gleaming with hatred. At last the figure was swallowed by the swirling fog.

When the phantom vanished over the crest of a hill, the farmers scattered to their cottages, unwilling to pursue the mystery. But ghoulish curiosity tempted two of them, and in the weeks that followed, they waited night after night by the road for the dismembered apparition. At last it appeared, its neck glistening wetly in the moonlight, and when it had drifted past, the men crept from the bushes to follow it.

It paid them no heed, although in their frightened haste they rustled the shrubbery and stumbled on the rutted lane. The farmers lagged many paces behind the figure as it glided up the hill and down into a neighboring glen, where it stopped at a well. There the phantom paused, its severed head swinging heavily against its back. It cast its burden down the well, and an instant after the splash, itself pitched forward down the shaft and vanished from sight. The farmers, watching from the hilltop, were startled to hear a second splash break the night stillness, as if the phantom were as weighty as any corpse.

When the farmers told their tale the next day, their hearers scoffed. But the

men of the village decided to search the well nonetheless, to lay the story to rest.

A ready village youth agreed to descend – with a lantern and a pole – in a sling fixed to the windlass. As he was winched down into the gloom, he saw nothing. Then dank vapors enveloped him, indicating that he was near the water. His lantern shimmered on the surface, and in its light, he discerned a long gray bundle, half-submerged. It gave when he prodded it.

He shouted up at the faces rimming the bright opening, and soon a second line, with a pothook tied to its end, trailed down into the well. The lad threaded the hook through the bundle's wrapping, gave another shout and was hauled up the well.

The carnival air of the crowd around the well vanished when the parcel was laid on the grass and its burlap wrapping undone. A mephitic stench rose from the bundle: There, with white bones starting from a mass of putrid flesh, were the remains of two legs, still shod in heavy boots.

The lad refused to venture down again, but a drunken fisherman volunteered to search the well for the rest of the corpse. He climbed into the sling and was lowered. At last a shout echoed from below. The men at the windlass strained to haul the fisherman up into daylight, and he appeared at the mouth of the well with a dark, dripping mass gathered in his arms.

He cast it to the ground and untangled himself from the sling, but the crowd kept its distance, forewarned this time by the stench. Standing over the sodden heap, the fisherman prodded it until it was recognizable. With a gurgle of revulsion, he backed away from what he had revealed: a legless corpse in an advanced state of decay. Its head, teeth showing through the eroded flesh of the cheeks, lolled freely, joined to the shoulders by a narrow flap of skin. In every detail, the corpse matched the ghost that the farmers had seen.

The onlookers guessed from the seaman's garb still shrouding the torso that the man had been a smuggler. The sheltered coves near Happisburgh received quantities of illicit silk, tobacco and spirits. His companions, they surmised, had slit his throat in a row, then hacked up his body so it would fit in the well. But the stench left the crowd with little will to speculate further. The minister and the undertaker were summoned, and the remains were buried with little ceremony.

And the ghost walked no more. Its business was done: It had captured the horrified gaze of the living and secured a proper burial for the corpse from which it sprang. In a sense the apparition was the most mild-mannered of ghosts, for it was animated not by a malicious desire to torment the living but by the simple need to communicate, to bear witness to a horrible crime and an unburied body.

Yet its terror remained. Much could be explained about its appearance and motives, but in the end the Happisburgh ghost was as chilling a puzzle as any other. However powerful the logic of a haunting, each is a rupture of the natural order in which death marks the end of earthly wanderings. The ultimate explanation for the walking dead lies forever hidden from the living, open to baffled mortals only when they too have slipped through the veil of death to join the spirit multitudes.

A Meeting on the Road Home

Late one March night in the English county of Lancashire, a man of average height and middle years left a tavern called the White Bull and headed down a narrow lane for home. His name was Gabriel Fisher and with him was his dog Trotty. Fisher was, perhaps, a little merrier than he had been during the day, but that night's journey was to sober him quickly.

A sickle moon cast its thin light down on tree and hedgerow; the evening was chilly, and Fisher walked along briskly enough, hearing little else but his own soft footfalls. As the man and his dog reached the midway point of their homeward journey, however, the silence was shattered by a high-pitched scream.

The dog began to whine. Fisher automatically ordered it to silence, and the sound of his own voice helped restore his courage. He peered into the gloom. On the road ahead was a figure, roughly human in form, though at that distance and in that light it was hard to say. Firmly gripping his walking staff, Fisher approached. The figure was a woman. She must have emitted

the scream herself—but why was a woman abroad at this hour, on this little-traveled road?

Even as he pondered this, his dog turned tail and fled. Fisher shouted after it, shrugged, then hurried to catch up with the woman, who had begun walking in the direction he himself was taking. She spoke not a word, and her bowed head was concealed by a large bonnet. Fisher drew up beside her and began to question her, but to his solicitous queries she made only the faintest replies. Yet her voice was somehow soothing—teasing, even, with a hint of lovely melody. He adjusted his long step to her shorter one and paced beside her down the road.

She carried a large, cloth-covered market basket, and after a moment, Fisher asked if he might carry it for her. She handed the basket to him, and he happily settled the wicker handle on his arm. The woman's gentle voice said, "You're much too kind." Then it broke into an unpleasantly mocking, tinkling laugh. Fisher looked in some surprise toward his companion, but she was turned away from him, apparently examining the hedge that bordered the road. The laugh sounded again, more loudly.

It came from the basket. Fisher stopped in his tracks and with a horrified oath flung the basket away. As he stared, it hit the ground, its cover fell away, and a head—whiter than the cloth that had concealed it—bounced out onto the road. Teeth shone in the wide-stretched mouth, from which issued a stream of cackling giggles. Fisher whirled to face his companion, who had turned toward him. Her bonnet had fallen back, her shoulders shook with soundless laughter, and she had no head.

Fisher leaped over the basket and took off down the road, running as he had not run since boyhood. Over the pounding of his heart he heard scuffling and then quick footsteps behind him. He ran on, his breath coming in loud sobs, and as he ran he looked back, only to see the arm of the woman raised high, lifting the head like a lantern.

The head laughed again, and she threw it after him. It struck the dirt and of its own accord sprang back into the air, whisking past Fisher, its eyes glittering and its teeth clacking.

When it again landed in the road, Fisher made an attempt to jump over it, but the head jumped too, snapping at his ankles. Once more the head passed him, then cut in front of his path and forced a second leap from Fisher, one that took his feet just clear of the vicious, biting grin. Fully caught up in its macabre sport now, the head played about his feet, snapping and laughing maniacally.

Fisher sped on, too terrified to tire or even to look back, although he realized that the woman and her head were close behind him. When he came to a shallow stream that ran across the road, he charged through it in an explosion of spray, then continued up a rise in the road.

As he crested the hill, Fisher cast a quick glance over his shoulder, and

the sight he saw in that one instant was impressed on his mind for the rest of his days. Below him, on the far side of the stream, stood a woman's figure, tall and stolid and headless still. Around its feet cavorted the head, snapping and snarling like some outlandish terrier. The hair of the head was caked with mud and the face blotched with dust, yet the head's baleful energy seemed to have reached a new pitch: Fisher could see its eyes blazing with malignity and hear a hellish echo in its cackling laughter.

Sick with loathing, he ran on. But he ran alone. The ghost, apparently limited in territory like others of its kind, could not cross running water.

Gabriel Fisher's adventure ended safely—even a little comically. He arrived home to find an irritable wife soothing the still-trembling Trotty. Her response to his stammered explanation was a barbed witticism. She said that she was glad he had learned the wisdom of coming home early, even though it had taken a headless woman to teach him. She, head and all, had never been able to make the point.

Others, too, scoffed when Gabriel recited his tale. But he was not the last person beset by the ghoul on that lonely stretch of road. Why the woman and her head patrolled there in the darkness, no one ever knew. Nor did they know precisely when the haunting ceased, for the people of Lancashire gave up all use of that narrow lane by night—and children would not venture there even in the daylight.

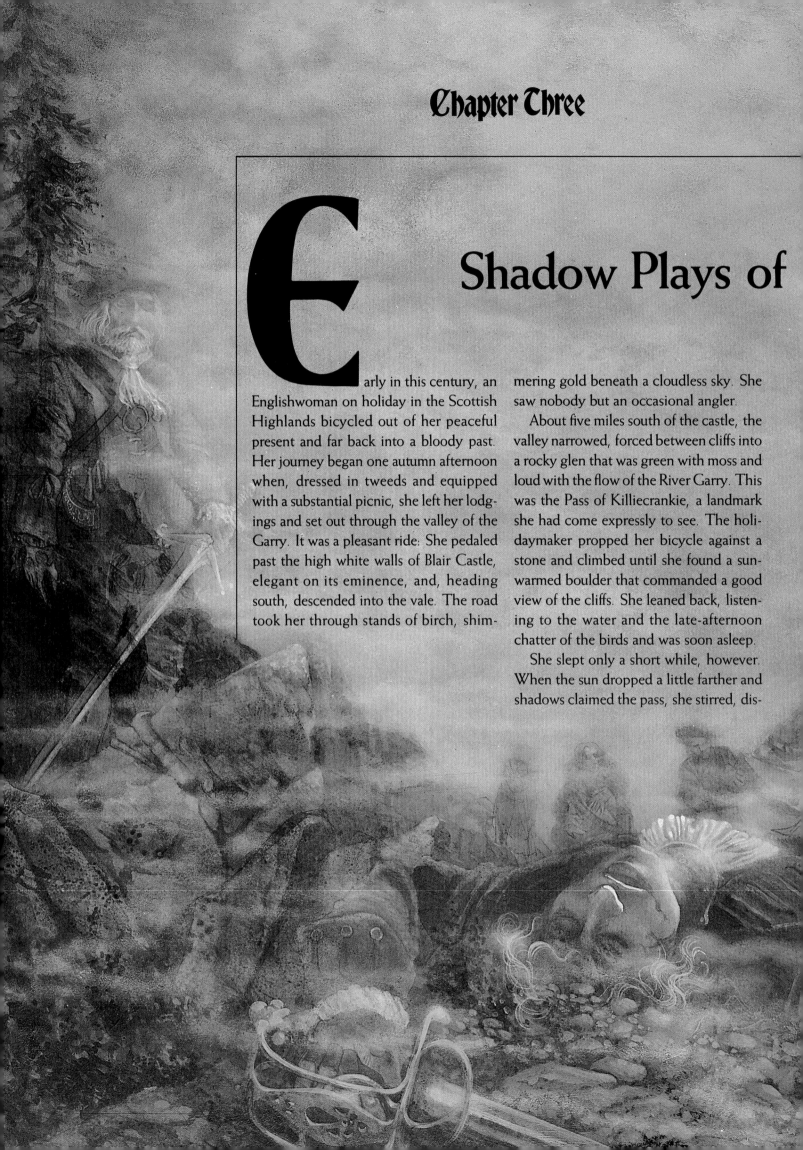

Chapter Three

Shadow Plays of

Early in this century, an Englishwoman on holiday in the Scottish Highlands bicycled out of her peaceful present and far back into a bloody past. Her journey began one autumn afternoon when, dressed in tweeds and equipped with a substantial picnic, she left her lodgings and set out through the valley of the Garry. It was a pleasant ride: She pedaled past the high white walls of Blair Castle, elegant on its eminence, and, heading south, descended into the vale. The road took her through stands of birch, shim-mering gold beneath a cloudless sky. She saw nobody but an occasional angler.

About five miles south of the castle, the valley narrowed, forced between cliffs into a rocky glen that was green with moss and loud with the flow of the River Garry. This was the Pass of Killiecrankie, a landmark she had come expressly to see. The holidaymaker propped her bicycle against a stone and climbed until she found a sun-warmed boulder that commanded a good view of the cliffs. She leaned back, listening to the water and the late-afternoon chatter of the birds and was soon asleep.

She slept only a short while, however. When the sun dropped a little farther and shadows claimed the pass, she stirred, dis-

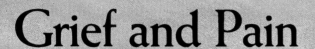

Grief and Pain

turbed by the chill. But she was disinclined to move. Why cycle miles in the dark when she could picnic on roast-beef sandwiches, lie in the heather-scented mountain air and repair to her hotel in the morning for a hearty breakfast? She was a practical woman and a seasoned traveler and she felt no anxiety about spending a night in the open. So she wrapped herself in her warm cloak and settled down to enjoy the evening. The sky's last glow faded, the stars appeared, and eventually she fell asleep again.

Hours later, she was awakened by a dull booming, suggestive of distant artillery. She sat up and looked around. The pass was silvered by moonlight so bright that she could clearly see the face of her wrist

watch. It was two o'clock in the morning. An owl called out.

Then, as she watched, the place came to life, evidently roused by the haunting cry of the bird. Clustered at the mouth of the valley of the Garry was a confused mass of red-coated men, fumbling with flintlocks and bayonets and crowded by heavily laden mules and horses. Swarming down upon them was a horde of Highlanders – huge, barefooted men clad in tartans and carrying shields and broadswords. They howled their battle cries as they charged, and the woman clearly heard the clan

names — Maclean and MacDonald and Cameron — and above the other calls, the name of King James.

The flintlocks popped raggedly but did nothing to slow the charge. Bayonets were even less effective. In a hideous rhythm, the Highlanders' broadswords rose and fell. The air was filled with cries of fear and pain, grunts, curses and pleas for God's aid in this desperate hour. Bodies splashed into the river and turned it red. Maimed soldiers writhed among the horses' hoofs, and the horses themselves screamed and thrashed in panic.

For long moments the carnage continued, hopelessly one-sided. Then, as the last red-coated soldier fell to Highland steel, the scene disappeared. Silence again held the valley.

But only briefly. As in a dream, a new scene appeared on the floor of the pass. It had become an abattoir: The rocky ground was strewn with twitching, broken bodies — and worse, with parts of bodies, limbs severed by the broadswords. Men lay where they had fallen, some staring flatly at the sky and others not staring at all, since they had no eyes to stare with. A few of these men moaned; one shrieked steadily, piercing the air with an unwavering, mindless sound. The stench was overwhelming. In the sky, eagles circled lazily, waiting for the coming feast.

The great birds did not descend, however, for other scavengers were busy on the battlefield. Bent figures scuttled among the bodies, plucking and pulling, fumbling and prying. It soon became clear who they were. Out of a tree not far from where the holidaymaker sat, a young woman dropped lightly to the ground and scrambled down the cliff. She was beautiful, in the dark fashion sometimes seen in the Highlands, and she wore a plaid shawl. On her arm she carried a large willow basket, and in her hand was a dirk — the sharp, broad-bladed dagger the Highlanders once kept sheathed in their stockings for use on game and humans alike.

Swiftly and methodically, the young woman moved among the bodies. She stripped off buttons and insignia, cut belts and pried off shoes. All these pickings were dropped into her basket. If a man moved or made a sound, she stabbed him through the heart or cut his throat with the same practiced ease she showed in harvesting valuables. If his ring refused to leave his finger, she severed the finger and dropped it into the basket as though it

were some vegetable yanked from the earth or twisted from a vine.

Her expression remained impassive throughout, until the Englishwoman, appalled, gave a choked cry. At once the dark maiden turned and, nimble as a cat, began to climb the rocks, her glittering eyes fixed on this new quarry.

The Englishwoman moaned, but she could not move. As helpless as a frightened child in a nightmare, she watched the predator ascend. At the moment that the white face loomed close, however, a wave of sickness swept over her, and merciful blackness closed in.

When she opened her eyes again, it was morning. The trees shivered in a fresh breeze; somewhere below, a bird sang. The pass was quiet and deserted save for herself; the river ran merrily over its rocky bed. Stiff and cold, she descended to her bicycle and slowly rode back across the golden valley of the Garry to her inn. There she bathed and breakfasted, and told her hosts what she had seen.

She was in no doubt about the nature of the action, and neither were they, for others had witnessed it over the years.

In the Pass of Killiecrankie in 1689, a terrible battle had taken place. The preceding year, the English had deposed James II, a Catholic and a Scot, and had set his daughter Mary and her Dutch husband, William of Orange, upon the throne. Scotland refused to accept the overthrow of James, and when British troops were sent to subdue the Highlands, a rabble of clans led by the brilliant John Graham, Viscount Dundee, slaughtered them. But it was the last such victory. Graham, called Bonnie Dundee, was killed in the encounter, and the Highlanders dispersed to their mountain fastness—but not before profiting from the kill. After the battle, said witnesses, the victors and their women plucked their victims clean.

The Pass of Killiecrankie was the most observant witness of all, it seemed. For some reason, the land watched and remembered. Every tree, leaf and stone was engraved with the images of the violence and the pain, and those memories were periodically shared with the living. Again and again, the ghostly armies clashed by night, and ghostly scavengers followed. In those events, there was something that death could never resolve or erase.

Many other such phantom battles have been reported over the centuries. On the chalk downs of Woodmanton in Wiltshire, where Briton fought Roman many generations before the battle at Killiecrankie, headless war horses used to gallop wildly through the night. At Glastonbury in Somerset—a holy place frequently defended—the ground sometimes shook with the footsteps of invisible marching armies. St. Albans in Hertfordshire was a battlefield twice in the 15th Century Wars of the Roses; for many years afterward, a house on that bloodied ground rang with the crash and clang of steel on steel.

Not surprisingly, the English Civil War had a full share of ghostly echoes. In October 1642, the first major battle and first Royalist defeat of that War occurred at Edgehill in Warwickshire. Four thousand men died. The following Christmas Eve,

Cotswold shepherds saw the deadly drama played out by specters. Terrified, they told their parson, and he joined them the next night. The men stood on a hill near the battlefield and heard in the night air the groans of dying men. Then, according to a later report, there "appeared in the air the same incorporeal soldiers that made these clamors and immediately, with ensigns displayed, drums beating, muskets going off, cannons discharged and horses neighing – which also to these men were visible – the alarum or entrance to this game of death was struck up." The entire battle was repeated, with all its thrusts, counterthrusts and roiling mayhem. A week later, witnesses sent by Charles I observed the same scene and even recognized the ghosts of their fallen comrades, including that of the King's standard-bearer. After that, the frequency of the spectral appearances decreased.

Britain had no monopoly on phantom warfare. Reports of apparitional armies are as old as war itself. Assyrian records speak of spectral bands assaulting desert cities as phantasmal as themselves. No doubt the battle cries of men long dead once floated over windy Troy and echoed on the plain at Marathon.

Battlefields, it seems, are places where earth, wood and stone absorb the spirits of the dying. Like photographic negatives, such sites retain the images of the people who expired there and can print those images again and again on the retinas of the living.

What the living see is not always readily decipherable. In the coal-mining Flintshire countryside of Wales, for example, people long puzzled over an apparition that haunted an earthen hummock set among the region's heaps of slag. Upon its crest, back and forth in measured pace, back and forth in strides that seemed timed to the heart's steady beat, marched the figure of an ancient man-at-arms.

Year after year, decade after decade, the spectral sentry maintained its solitary vigil, and on nights so dark that even the owls were blind, its armor could be seen to gleam with a golden sheen. At last, in the spirit of scientific inquiry that flourished at the beginning of the 19th Century, archeologists were drawn to the hillock where the apparition stood guard. As the scientists had suspected, the mound turned out to be a funeral barrow. When excavated, it surrendered, amid a helter-skelter of human bones, the intact skeleton of a tall man wearing a bronze corselet. The armor was overlaid with gold.

The protective garment was of Etruscan design, a style popular among the Roman legionaries who, in the First Century A.D., had surged into the south of Wales, only to be fought to a temporary standstill by Caratacus, the much-honored chieftain of the tribes that lived there. Near the site of the barrow, the centurion in golden armor had doubtless fallen in some forgotten battle, and his spirit had walked ever since as a sentinel to safeguard the sleep of his comrades in their shared grave.

Be that as it may, the skeleton in its fine array was removed to a place of honor in the British Museum and, instead of a coffin, was given a glass case, in which it may

Some tales of haunted rooms are long, but many more are short, and the shortest tale of all concerns a man startled from a deep sleep. He lay in a pitch-dark, silent room and longed for the comfort of a lighted candle. The story runs, in its entirety, as follows: "He woke up frightened and reached for a match, and a match was put into his hand."

A chill touch in the night

Gilsland Castle in Cumberland was a forbidding place, its stone walls shining with dampness, its dark corridors swept by icy drafts. Once a small boy was shut in an empty upstairs room as a punishment for mischief. The lad froze to death there, and for centuries afterward, his little nightgowned figure could be seen wandering the house, upstairs and downstairs and at the door of every chamber. Teeth chattering, body trembling, he walked the dark, searching for an open door. If he entered a room where someone was sleeping, he merely whimpered by the bed. If the person was ill, he would lay his frigid hand upon the sufferer and whisper, "Cold, cold, forever cold. You shall be cold forever more." The invalid always died after that visitation, eased out of pain by the touch of the Cold Lad of Gilsland Castle.

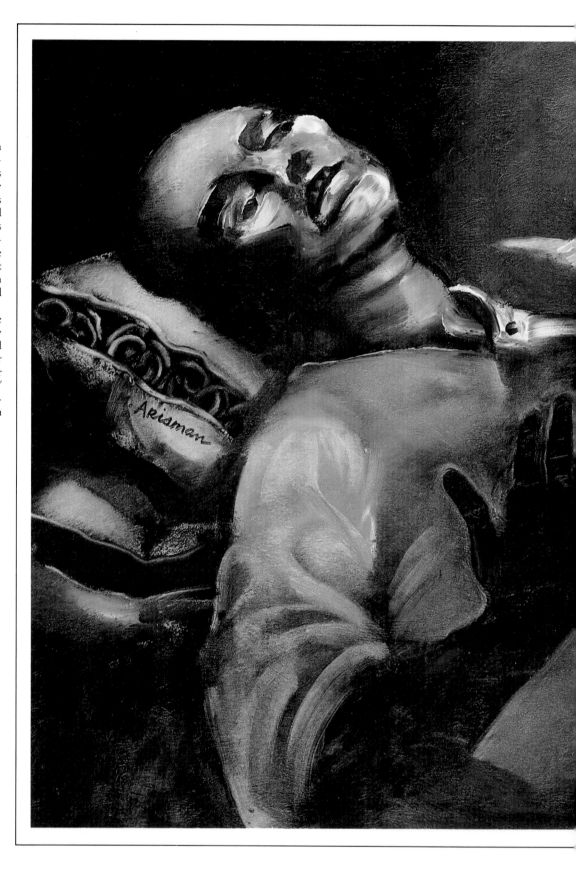

still be viewed. With the razing of the barrow and the removal of its mortal remains, the ghost disappeared, relieved of its duty after fourteen hundred years.

History has spawned many haunted places other than battlefields: Wherever violence was concentrated, ghosts could stake a claim. The Celts were prodigal in creating such sites. They practiced human sacrifice, sometimes to propitiate their bloodthirsty gods at seasonal festivals, sometimes as an aid to divination, a fact recorded by the Second Century B.C. Greek historian Posidonius in an account of his travels in Gaul. He observed that the Druidic priests of the Celts foretold the patterns of the future by the writhings of their human sacrifices.

The sacred groves in which these rites were performed were places of horror. One discovered near Marseilles was described by the Roman writer Marcus Annaeus Lucanus, better known as Lucan. Among the trees of the grove, shadow reigned; the gods' altars – "stark, gloomy blocks of unworked timber, rotten with age" – lurked in the leafy darkness. "The barbaric gods worshipped here had their altars heaped with hideous offerings, and every tree was sprinkled with human blood." Lucan added that the Celts shunned the grove, fearing it haunted. Perhaps the Romans shared that fear; in any event, they found the barbarians' sacrificial practices outrageous, and they destroyed the grove – and presumably any others they came across.

In some cases, the responsibility for long-ago paroxysms of cruelty is unclear.

During the last century, for example, residents of Reculver, on the coast of Kent, became convinced that something awful had once happened at a fortress there. The fortress was in ruins, sealing within its layered debris the evidence of successive waves of conquest and habitation by Celts, Romans and Saxons. Around it on stormy nights could be heard the weeping of babies, a heart-rending whimpering and sobbing that went on hour after hour, rising and falling in the dark. This haunting continued for many years, and people avoided the place, for they were helpless to ease such suffering. But the site was eventually excavated, and in it was found a jumble of infants' skeletons, the remains of babies buried alive, scholars thought, for some early sacrifice. But precisely who did it or why, the scholars could not say.

In better-documented eras, hauntings have often been associated with places of secular execution – not only the humble gallows and the scaffold, but also prisons where the mighty met their ends. Berkeley Castle, rising gray and bleak from its Gloucestershire water meadows, long reverberated with the anguished howls of the damned because of a horrible murder that was done there. The weak Plantagenet King, Edward II, himself a blot on the besmirched 14th Century, was killed in a cell in the castle – spitted on a red-hot poker by the order of his wife, Isabella of France. But Isabella met a ghastly fate, too. Imprisoned at Castle Rising in Norfolk for the murder, she went mad. Throughout every day of life that remained to her, she shrieked and ranted and tore at her flesh. And for centuries after she died, the

echoes of her screams sounded on the stone stairs under the arches leading to the keep where she was held.

The list of such haunted places is long indeed. Some castles contain not one but several ghosts engendered by murders or executions; some, like Glamis in Scotland, are home to as many as nine (*page 85*). But one place stands out. No stronghold shelters as many of the restless dead as the Tower of London, that fortress-prison on the banks of the Thames.

Sited on a hill, the fortress is so massive that it seems too heavy for its plot of earth. It is ringed with defenses – a moat and two tall, concentric, many-towered curtain walls. The towers in the walls – the Bloody Tower, the Salt Tower, Beauchamp Tower – hold prison cells, oppressive chambers whose breath has been crushed out by the weight of the stone that forms them. They are reached by dark and narrow stairs that seem to have been tunneled through living rock. On those sweating prison walls are scratched the words of prisoners who languished and perished there – a motley of prayers and protests, monograms and names.

The prison towers surround the heart of the fortress, William the Conquerer's four-turreted White Tower, ninety feet high and nine centuries old. In this tower's crypt once were torture chambers. At its base, on the placid, well-groomed patch of grass called Tower Green, the executioner's block once stood. Beneath that pretty greensward – and beneath the floor of the chapel of St. Peter ad Vincula, which stands beside it – lay the bones of hundreds of the headless dead.

Besides being a prison, the Tower has served at various times as a barracks, an armory and occasionally as a royal palace. During the day, although forbidding in mien, it was always bustling and busy. But at dusk, when the gates were closed and locked and the keys given into the chief warden's safekeeping, the castle slowly changed in character. The shadows lengthened on the stone walls; Tower Green faded to a square of black. The ravens that strutted there ceased their harsh calling, and the voices of the garrison sounded only faintly from the barracks. In the darkness, silence settled on the Inner Ward, broken only by the measured footsteps of the sentries who paced the leads and by the soft commands they gave to mark the watches of the night.

They did not walk alone, however, and they knew it. The ghosts of those whose bodies nourished the grass of Tower Green and crowded the floor in front of the altar of St. Peter ad Vincula emerged when day was done, and walked where they had walked before. Late in the 15th Century, for instance, guards passing the stair of the Bloody Tower saw what seemed to be a pair of shadows moving slowly along the walls. They were the size of children, and they were holding hands. Mild and wordless, the little apparitions glided down the staircase and disappeared.

In the speculations set off by this visitation, most people identified the shadows as the ghosts of Edward and Richard Plantagenet, imprisoned and presumably murdered in the Tower in 1483, during the

What the brewer saw

Long ago, a house in west Cornwall called Trewoof came to be haunted by the ghosts of two mistresses of the owner – his housekeeper and a younger rival she had poisoned. The younger ghost resided quietly in the room where she had died, but that of the housekeeper terrorized the place until an exorcist confined it in the same room and gave it the task of eternally carding wool. Then the door was shut upon the pair forever.

In later times, few people remembered the details of these events, although gossips sometimes pointed to a little window in the eaves above the house's brewing chambers and repeated the old tale that ghosts were imprisoned behind it. But there was no way of knowing for sure. During many alterations to the upper floors, the room to which the window belonged had been sealed off, its door plastered shut and incorporated into a wall.

Late one October night, however, a man working in the brewing chambers heard clicking noises overhead. Curious, he tapped on the ceiling with his malt shovel. His taps were returned. He went to investigate.

The brewer propped a ladder beneath the little window in the eaves, climbed up and peered through the dusty panes into a dimly lighted room. It appeared to be filled with rubbish – but the rubbish was moving.

As his eyes adjusted, he realized that he was looking at a heap of black wool, and in it sat a lumpish creature, its massive head weighted with matted hair, its hands moving rhythmically, pulling shreds of wool through a carding comb. This was the housekeeper of the old tale, and in the next instant, the brewer saw the companion ghost – a meager thing, scabrous with the blue marks of poison. The pair stared at the window, cackling and beckoning.

The brewer lost his footing and fell. He was alive when he was found, and he related what he had seen. But having looked into the eyes of the ghosts, he knew he must shortly die. And he did, within the week.

dynastic struggles of the Wars of the Roses. It was whispered that they had been killed by the order of their uncle who, once the boys were dead and their superior claim to the throne dispensed with, could take the crown as Richard III. This never was conclusively proved, and the nameless shades continued to appear for almost two hundred years. But in the 17th Century, two small skeletons – thought to be those of the boy Princes – were discovered near the Bloody Tower and interred in Westminster Abbey. After this, the pathetic specters vanished for good.

They had a plethora of successors, however, most of them provided by the politically bloody reigns of the Tudors. The earliest Tudor ghosts were not drifting phantoms but actors in a violent scene replayed at night before the terrified eyes of castle wardens. In the hours of the last watch, before the dawn broke over Tower Hill, the executioner's block, phantasmal yet solid-looking, appeared in the center of Tower Green. It was flanked by two apparitions: an elderly woman dressed in the puffed sleeves and the stiff, brocaded skirts of an earlier time, and her executioner, a burly man hidden in a black hood.

The executioner dragged the woman to the steps of the block. Then screaming began. Wrenching herself from his grasp, the woman cried, "My head never committed treason. If you want it, you must take it if you can." And she bolted.

Round and round the green she ran, panting like an animal, weaving and dodging, with the executioner at her heels. He swung his shining ax as he ran – at the woman's shoulder, at her back, at her head – and each time he did so, blood spurted and the woman screamed again. At last she stumbled to her knees, her blood-drenched hair spread about her shoulders. Once more, the executioner dragged her to the block; she was now too weak to resist him. He raised the ax and brought it down on her neck, and the head rolled free. At that point, block, woman and executioner disappeared from view.

The actual butchery, historians agreed, took place in 1541, at the execution of the Countess of Salisbury. True to her protests, this doughty woman had not committed treason, but she was the mother of Cardinal Pole, who steadfastly opposed Henry VIII's separation from the Church of Rome. The Cardinal fled to Rome to escape the King's wrath, so the King, in his customary fashion, let the rest of the family feel the weight of his royal displeasure.

Other Tudor ghosts appeared from time to time on the Tower grounds. Among them was the white figure of Lady Jane Grey, the Nine Days' Queen, who appeared each February 12, the anniversary of her execution in 1554. At seventeen, this poor victim of parental ambition – wrongly set on the throne that belonged to Mary Tudor – watched from the window of her prison chamber while her young husband rode to his execution, and watched again as his headless corpse, wrapped in a scarlet-stained sheet, returned in a cart. All the while she heard the sound of hammering on Tower Green, where workmen were constructing her own scaffold – a platform built high, so that witnesses might clearly see the beheading. She went to her death meekly, reciting the Miserere—"Have mercy upon me, O God." The witnesses commented that the torrent of blood was extraordinary for such a small body.

A ghost of another generation that sometimes walked the halls of the Tower was that of Sir Walter Raleigh, who spent thirteen comfortable years incarcerated there. He was allowed the company of his wife and produced both his *History of the World* and a son while imprisoned. But at last he too went to the block, suspected by Elizabeth I of treasonous plotting.

Of all these shades, however, none captured the public imagination so firmly as that of Anne Boleyn, second wife of the much-married Henry VIII and mother of Elizabeth. Henry had her beheaded on charges of adultery and incest—probably trumped up, since the King no longer had use for her. On a fine May morning in 1536 she went to death gaily, dressed in a gown of damask and a scarlet petticoat. She wore a pearl headdress on her shining hair. With typical panache, she had declared that she had a "little, little neck," too fine to be dealt with by the ax-wielding executioner of the Tower; she was beheaded by a specially trained French swordsman. "This lady," the Governor of the Tower remarked, "has much joy and pleasure in death." The headless corpse was crammed into an arrow case and buried under the floor of St. Peter ad Vincula.

But Anne Boleyn was far too vivacious to rest for long, and her ghost flitted about the Tower grounds for years afterward. As late as the 19th Century, it became the focus of a much-discussed incident.

This occurred one night when an officer of the guard stopped a sentry on his rounds and inquired about a light he had seen streaming from the windows of the chapel—a soft, unusual and quite unauthorized light. The sentry, who had walked this round many times, replied that he did not know what produced the light but that it was often seen. He was plainly reluctant to pursue the matter. The officer then tried the doors of the chapel. Finding them locked, he propped a ladder to a window, climbed it and peered in.

The pretty, late-Perpendicular interior shone with candlelight, and in the golden glow, a splendid company of gentlemen and ladies moved. Blazing in the silks and bejeweled ornaments of the Tudor court, they wound through the chapel and up the aisle toward the altar, where one by one they sank silently into the floor. As the last one disappeared, the light faded and the chapel was left in darkness. But the officer had recognized the proudest one among them from her portraits; it was, of course, Queen Anne.

Shortly after this incident, the floor of the chapel was dug up. More than two hundred skeletons, including that of the hapless Queen, were found.

Anne Boleyn appeared many other times as the years passed by. Generally she was headless, as in death. One sentry was said to have died of fright, and another to have been court-martialed for fainting on duty, when her shade—ignoring the challenge that he bravely made—

Haggard and shaken, an English country-house guest once enthralled his breakfast companions with this account of his night's adventure: His hostess had warned him, he said, that his bedchamber was haunted, but he had merely laughed at this. When he went up the stairs to his bedchamber that night, however, he found himself anxious—unaccountably so, for the room was well lighted and eminently comfortable. To soothe his nerves, he looked under the bed and into each cupboard. He examined the blanket chest and opened every drawer of every table. All was serene: He was alone in the room. After a glance up and down the empty hallway, he closed the bedchamber door and bolted it. Then he shut the windows, latched them, drew the curtains and snuffed out all the candles but one. Then he got into bed, pulled the covers to his chin and lay there as still as he could, listening. He heard nothing, not a rustle, not a murmur. Relaxed at last, he extinguished the bedside candle, and as he did so, he heard a voice—a tiny, dry, satisfied voice that seemed to emanate from an inkstand on the desk. It spoke only once, but that was enough to keep him in a state of rigid wakefulness until dawn. "Now we're shut in for the night," it said.

walked through him. (Only the testimony of others who had seen the apparition saved him from punishment.) But never again did a living person see the Queen as richly dressed and as darkly beautiful as she had been at the height of her power, when she shone in Henry's favor.

The slaughtered, the sacrificed, the executed—all those who died by some extreme of violence or heartlessness—seemed to imbue the place of their passing with a kind of latent energy, a stored stress that found periodic release in ghostly emanations. But such stress was not always built into a place in a single horrific burst. It could also be stored up over a long period. For this reason, the most common of haunted sites were not battlefields or prisons but houses, the homes that people built and lived their lives in. The word "haunt," in fact, derives from the same Old English root as the word "home"; "haunt" means literally "to fetch home."

A house, after all, has always been more than a roof that shelters and a hearth that offers warmth. It is also a physical manifestation of those who dwell within. Everything in the home, from the pictures on the walls to the humblest pots and pans, is part and record of the people living there, molded by their presence. In a spiritual as well as a material sense, the house is them, and this mingling of identities is never entirely lost.

But a house does not stand alone, free of outside influence. Throughout human history, people have felt a need to supply their homes with protections against misfortune and evil. As recently as the 19th Century, it was a custom in Europe to endow a building with good fortune by incorporating bread (the staff of life) and salt (symbol of purity) in the foundation. In earlier, pagan times, much stranger measures were commonly used. It was thought that constructing a house disturbed the gods of the earth beneath. The gods had to be propitiated by blood sacrifice; otherwise, the house would not stand.

Sometimes the sacrifices were human, as the discovery of skeletons and skulls immured in the foundations of various European buildings attests; it is possible that the infants found at Reculver were buried alive to ensure the structure's safety. And sacrifice had another purpose besides placating the earth gods. The ghost of the person sacrificed, it was thought, would haunt the place forever, serving as a guardian against the intrusion of hostile ghosts.

As civilization progressed, the idea of human sacrifice became repugnant, and substitutions were made. William the Conqueror, it was said, had bulls' blood mixed into the mortar during the construction of the Tower of London. Ordinary houses often had the carcasses of chickens, cats and other animals put in the walls or foundation during the building. The custom was common enough in Scandinavia—in church as well as house construction—that ghosts of the sacrificed animals were given a special name: *kirkevarer*, or "church wares" or "church inhabitants." The animal chosen might be the first one that wandered near the building site; more often, it was a lamb, and it was buried beneath the (continued on page 91)

The Phantom
Tenants of
Castle Glamis

A vision of stony dignity, Castle Glamis looms proudly above Scotland's Angus countryside, giving no outward sign of the troubles it has known — and may know still, if tales about its phantoms are true. At its core stands a massive structure called the Square Tower. Secret chambers lie within the tower, it is said, and they hold ghosts of generations of the Lyon family — lords of Glamis since the 14th Century. As with the records of many noble families, the story of the Earls of Strathmore — the Lyons' best-known title — has dark chapters along with the bright. Some of what went on within the castle's walls has been blurred by time, and some may have been concealed. It was rumored, for example, that a hidden room in the tower imprisoned a monster. The creature was variously thought to be a half-human progeny of a long-dead Earl of Strathmore, or a vampire-like being that periodically appeared in the family line, or the ghost of either one. In any case, the gossips said, it was known to three people in each generation: the incumbent earl, his heir and his steward, and they revealed details to no one. But a 19th Century visitor to the castle saw the monster. The visitor was a stolid young woman, curious

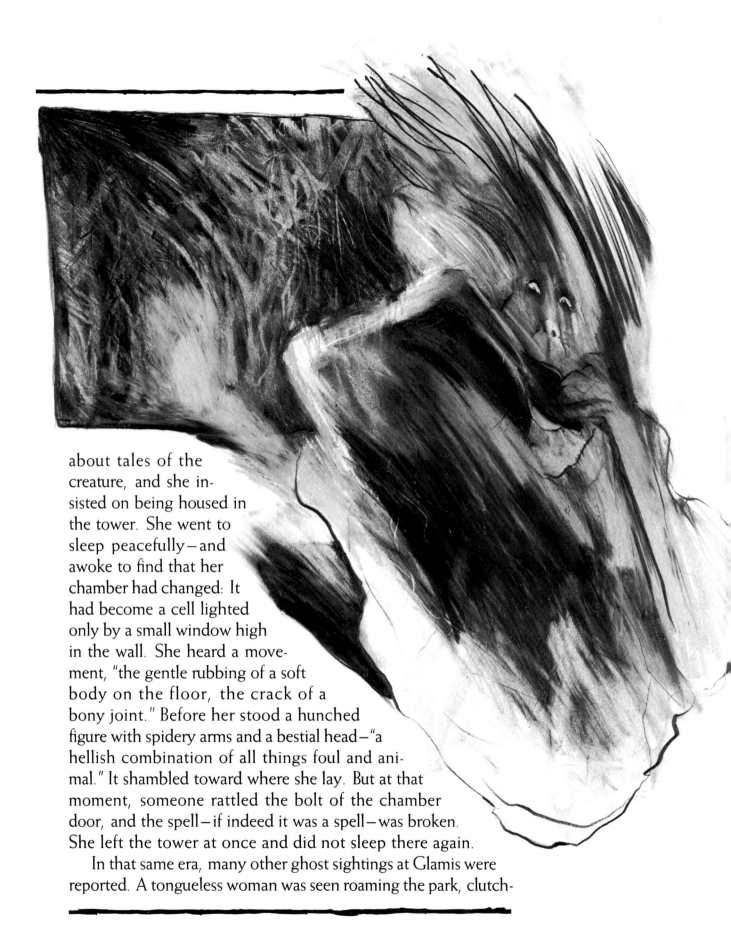

about tales of the creature, and she insisted on being housed in the tower. She went to sleep peacefully—and awoke to find that her chamber had changed: It had become a cell lighted only by a small window high in the wall. She heard a movement, "the gentle rubbing of a soft body on the floor, the crack of a bony joint." Before her stood a hunched figure with spidery arms and a bestial head—"a hellish combination of all things foul and animal." It shambled toward where she lay. But at that moment, someone rattled the bolt of the chamber door, and the spell—if indeed it was a spell—was broken. She left the tower at once and did not sleep there again.

In that same era, many other ghost sightings at Glamis were reported. A tongueless woman was seen roaming the park, clutching at her bleeding mouth. A white lady drifted through the corridors. And a tiny page sometimes appeared outside the state apartments. Still, interest remained centered on the Square Tower and the unearthly noises heard there. Some people believed that a secret chamber—never discovered—housed the gnawed skeletons and pleading ghosts of sixteen members of the Ogilvy clan who, during a 17th Century feud, sought shelter in the castle. The lord of that time locked them in the tower and unaccountably left them to starve. But death did not silence them: In after years, their cries echoed along the stone walls and resounded among the rafters.

More often, the noise that rent the Square Tower was attributed to the activities of the first Lord Glamis, a rakehell so vicious that he was commonly known as the Wicked Laird. Gambling was his passion, and his taste for drink was equally immoderate. One stormy Sabbath

night, finding himself without a card partner, he retired to his room in a rage, swearing that he would play with the devil himself. Almost at once, the door swung open and a tall stranger entered the room. With a courteous smile, he offered his services.

The laird agreed, and the two sat down to play. Drawn by their noise—for they played a raucous game—a servant crept up the stairs and put his eye to the keyhole. At once, the stranger turned from his cards and pointed at the door. From his finger leaped a needle of light; it stabbed across the room, through the keyhole and into the eye of the spy. When the servant cried out, the

Brian M'Eall

Wicked Laird turned, and in that instant, the stranger disappeared, having just moments before won the soul of his opponent. The laird lived on for five more years, but on the anniversary of the game—to the very hour—the devil came to claim him. After the death of the Wicked Laird, however, his ghost regularly appeared in his bedchamber, playing cards with the devil in death as he had in life. The noise was so distressing that his descendants had the room walled up.

Or so some stories say. Of the various ghosts that haunted Glamis, the laird was remembered particularly well, perhaps because he seems to have cursed his immediate descendants. Among the males, one died in a duel, one in a brawl, another in an uprising and still another mysteriously while dining alone—poisoned, it was said, by his wife. Several years later, she was tried for witchcraft and burned. Some people say that she walks Glamis to this day, as does one of the earls—no one is quite sure which. He appears late at night on the battlements and is simply called the Mad Earl.

altar. To see its small ghost wandering in the night in the churchyard or between the rows of pews meant death.

In the Middle Ages, a different sort of substitute was used in areas as far apart as the Slavic countries and the British Isles: Buildings were protected by trapping human shadows in the foundations. The origin of this practice lay in the ancient belief that a person's shadow – that curious companion, sometimes visible and mimicking every movement, sometimes hidden – was his soul. A shadow buried in a building could therefore serve the same protective function as a sacrificial victim.

The idea led to some unpleasant practices, only dimly remembered now. It was said that in Rumania, master builders in remote villages would induce strangers to approach building sites and stand in such a way that their shadows fell on the spot destined for the foundation stone. Some builders patronized grim specialists in protection: shadow merchants. These furtive tradesmen contrived to measure the length of an unsuspecting person's shadow by dropping a cord or rod upon it when it lay on the ground. Measurement by this technique was thought to trap the shadow; the measuring device was then sold to a builder and buried in a foundation. Such commerce, far from being a humane alternative to sacrifice, was tantamount to murder: It was believed that anyone robbed of his soul would waste away and die, without ever discovering what ailed him.

The guarding of houses did not occur only during the construction phase. Finished houses, too, were surrounded with protections, especially at the doors. The Celts, who believed that strength and soul remained in the head after death, suspended the skulls of conquered enemies from their house walls or set them in niches to serve as defenders.

Less grisly guardians came from the plant world. Sprigs of rowan – long considered a protective tree – once commonly decorated English door lintels. An even more widespread protector was the houseleek, planted on roofs all over Europe. Called in Latin *Sempervivum*, or "ever living," this evergreen succulent consists of a rosette-shaped parent plant that continually reproduces itself by sending out offsets – miniature rosettes with their own root systems; the visual effect gives the plant its common name, hen and chickens. The houseleek was a sacred symbol of Zeus in Mediterranean countries and of Thor in Teutonic ones. People believed that it warded off lightning and evil spirits. In England, village folk warned that its flowers must never be plucked from a roof, lest the occupants of the house die.

And of course, iron always served as a shield against spirits of the other world. It might take the form of a horseshoe suspended over a door. It might be scissors, opened to form a cross and placed under the threshold. Or it might even be a hideous, cast-iron face that served as a door knocker, as scowling and menacing as any Celtic skull.

While all of these various protections were considered efficacious against witches and demons and hostile ghosts, they were not meant to prevent the appearance of ghosts that belonged to a house, whose sight and breath and voices had been absorbed by the walls themselves. At the moment of death and at burial, measures were taken to hasten the newly dead into the other world (*page 112*), but no tactic was foolproof. Given the strength of the bond between people and their homes, a visitation from the grave was always possible. The Irish, surmising that festive occasions would exert an especially strong pull on the departed, put cups of milk on the windowsills as refreshment for family ghosts who might return on Christmas Eve.

Familial hauntings were particularly common in Scandinavia, where the dead were frequently seen going about the usual business of the lives they had left behind. There were tales of dead farmers observed at night foddering the animals in the barns — to no effect, it was said, for the animals remained hungry. And there were poignant stories of visits by the ghosts of old people — a dead grandmother anxiously feeling new wallpaper that had been hung in her parlor, or a poor old couple walking arm in arm from the churchyard to their tiny cottage, where they sat together in the single small room, feeding clods of peat to a stove in which no fire burned.

A curious characteristic of many Scandinavian house ghosts was their malevolence, which may have been caused by envy. No matter how affectionate some people were in life, their ghosts seemed full of malice and mockery toward the living. Thus, mourners would return from funerals to find their just-dead relatives squatting in the cow byre or straddling the roof beam and grinning maliciously all the while. Even worse were ghosts who sneered at the living and parroted their words in a mindless, maddening way Such ghosts required exorcism by priests.

But apart from Scandinavia, outright animosity toward the living seemed rare in house ghosts. Most appeared to be oblivious of those they shared quarters with. Bodiless shades, they simply drifted through their former homes or — if they had been guilty or unhappy people — reenacted scenes from their lives. Although they startled the living, they did no harm.

Such a one appeared quite frequently at Bisham Abbey, a handsome English country house in Berkshire. By doing so, the ghost revealed a crime that its perpetrator had thought to conceal. Or so the evidence would suggest.

During the reign of Elizabeth I, the house served as the county seat of Sir Thomas Hoby, by then famous for his elegant translation of that monument to High Renaissance manners and values, Baldassare Castiglione's *Il Cortegiano — The Courtier*. Hoby lived at Bisham with his wife, Dame Elizabeth, who was a scholar in her own right. The couple's life together would seem to have been distinguished and quiet. Yet after Dame Elizabeth died, her ghost frequently was seen walking the halls of Bisham Abbey, carrying a basin and evidently attempting, endlessly and futilely, to wash its hands.

The ghost was observed as late as the 19th Century — and by a man who did not believe in hauntings. He was a Naval officer — an admiral, in fact — and Bisham Abbey by then had come into his possession. One day he was alone in the great hall of the house, studying a portrait of Dame Elizabeth. Even on canvas, she had a vivid and imposing presence: She wore a black gown with a snowy lace stomacher and ruff; her face was framed by a pleated white veil; her hands were slender and long-fingered, in the style so highly regarded during Elizabeth's reign.

The admiral gazed thoughtfully at the portrait, and it returned his gaze, as portraits sometimes seem to do. All was still, yet the man sensed a movement at his back. He turned. Dame Elizabeth Hoby stood in the hall behind him. With a sad, backward glance she drifted toward the door, passed through and vanished.

It certainly appeared to be Dame Elizabeth, but in curious guise: The black gown was white and the white lace black, as if in a photographic negative. The admiral looked at the beautiful portrait to confirm his impression—and saw that the picture frame was empty. Disoriented, wondering about his sanity, he passed his hand in front of his eyes. As soon as he looked again, the portrait had reappeared.

Neither the admiral nor any of those who saw the lady's mournful shade knew why Dame Elizabeth roamed Bisham Abbey. But the gossips told this story:

Late in her childbearing years, Dame Elizabeth gave birth to a son whom she and Sir Thomas named William. Posterity knows little of William except that he was apparently slow of mind and untidy of habit, especially when compared with Lady Elizabeth's other two sons, Edward and Thomas—both of whom were eventually to earn knighthood—and her daughters, Elizabeth and Ann.

Dame Elizabeth was known not only for her learning but for the unbridled contempt she showed toward stupidity and slovenliness. She also had an explosive temper. When her dull-witted son tried and failed to do his lessons, and then failed again, Dame Elizabeth beat him.

Harsh treatment of the young was common in Tudor times; parents had what amounted to absolute authority over their children. Poor Lady Jane Grey told the scholar Roger Ascham that her parents required such complete perfection of her and treated her smallest failures so brutally that she thought herself in hell when she was with them. The only surcease she had was the company of her tutor. But Dame Elizabeth's behavior was unusual even then: William died from her beatings.

The Hoby family evidently conspired, under Dame Elizabeth's iron guidance, to hide the tragedy. No William appears in the family records of that time. His name is missing from the family's funeral monument in Bisham Church. For all that timeworn stone or yellowed vellum can show, William never existed.

Yet rumors persisted that Dame Elizabeth had delivered a fifth child, that it had survived infancy and then, some years later, had vanished. Rumor even claimed that the child had been killed. Such speculation would have ceased after Dame Elizabeth's death, if her specter had not continued to walk the abbey in torment.

And something else fed the gossip. It

was said that Dame Elizabeth had overlooked a piece of mundane evidence. Some years after she died, the house was refurbished, and in the course of construction, workmen supposedly discovered a cache of school supplies hidden behind a baseboard. There were slates, hornbooks and small sheets of paper. The lessons that could be deciphered were untidily written, but on one of them could be discerned a childishly scrawled name – William Hoby.

A sad tale indeed was that of William Hoby. Most house hauntings are sad, if not because they recall violence, guilt and grief, then because they seem to represent a wistful longing for what can no longer be. The poignance of haunting is that of mortality, the mortal's understanding that

Europe once abounded in haunted houses and haunted battlefields; Rome had a haunted bridge – the Ponte Sisto, which spans the Tiber not far from the Farnese Palace. On dark nights, loiterers on the quay of the Lungotevere dei Vallati often saw a black coach thunder across the bridge and down the bank, disappearing into the river. The coach was drawn by black horses, and coach and horses were wreathed in the flames of perdition. Inside rode a shriveled old woman, clutching two coffers of gold.

This was the ghost of Olimpia Maidalchini Pamphili, sister-in-law of Pope Innocent X. In her lifetime, an anagram had been made of her name: "Olim Pia, Nunc Impia" – "Once Pious, Now Impious." Some people referred to her as "Papessa" because of her iron control of her brother-in-law, whose mistress she was said to be.

Her treatment of Innocent was cold and cruel, right to his dying day. When the Pope lay mortally ill, Donna Olimpia, who had become immensely rich at the papacy's expense, stole into his chamber and took two coffers of gold from under his bed. She told no one that he was dying, and Innocent expired alone, covered only by a single thin blanket. But when Donna Olimpia died in her turn, she paid for the callous deed. Forever after, her ghost hurtled across the Tiber in breakneck flight – a frantic journey that invariably led to hell.

even the moments filled with laughter are only moments. They come and are and pass away, leaving only an image in the memory and a whisper of what was.

Such lingering sadness pervades the palace of Versailles, a house built as a reflection of one man's might. In the 17th Century, Louis XIV, with the aid of France's most distinguished architects, transformed a small and rustic château fourteen miles from Paris into a majestic complex of buildings spread over fifty-seven square miles of park and woodland. The grounds were designed so that, no matter where the eye looked, it was interested, charmed, pleased and awed. In hundreds of fountains, marble nymphs forever played; in innumerable still sheets of water, gilded Apollos forever rode chariots of the sun. And hidden away on the vast estates were smaller jewel-like châteaux, built for the retreat of "the Sun King" and his descendants. Among these satellite châteaux were the elegant Marly, the suave Grand Trianon and that vision of grace, the Petit Trianon.

The last, standing serene in a miniature park, was commissioned by the Sun King's heir, Louis XV, to house his mistresses, but its most famous occupant was the 18th Century Queen, Marie Antoinette. Here, insulated from the economic troubles and social discord besetting France, the Royal Family and the courtiers whiled away the days in parties, games and other frivolities. The place is quiet and somehow bereft now, a relic of an age of elegance.

At the turn of this century, however, two Englishwomen visiting the Petit Trianon found much more than a monument to the pleasures of the Old Regime. They made a record of their adventure.

The women were an unlikely pair to be meeting with spirits. Anne Moberly and Eleanor Jourdain were distinguished scholars who both served as principals of St. Hugh's College, Oxford. It happened that Miss Jourdain had a flat in Paris, where she tutored young Englishwomen, giving a final Continental polish to their education. Miss Moberly, free on a summer holiday, paid a visit, and one August morning, the pair went to see Versailles, where neither had been before.

Armed with their guidebook, they strolled among the splendors: the Hall of Mirrors, ablaze with gold; the tapestry-adorned royal apartments; the painted salons. At last, however, surfeited by the richness and tempted by the summer day, they set out through the palace gardens.

Down tree-lined avenues they proceeded, past the Orangerie with its rows of tidy trees in tubs, toward the Petit Trianon, whose relatively intimate elegance seemed more suited to their mood than the majesty of Louis XIV's great house. The day was cloudy; a breeze brushed past them, carrying the scent of flowers.

The women passed the Grand Trianon and entered the broad drive that, according to their map, led to the smaller palace. Miss Jourdain, however, saw a narrow, pleasant-looking path branching off and leading into the trees. The ladies chose to follow it.

They strolled through a wood and into a clearing, where a house, a barn and assorted outbuildings stood. A plow leaned against one of the walls. In a window, Miss Moberly glimpsed a woman shaking out a white cloth. Miss Jourdain did not see the woman; in fact, she later recalled thinking just then that the buildings were deserted. (Their memories of these events, set down with scholarly meticulousness, would differ in a number of small details.)

Both women felt a deepening sadness and depression. The place seemed lifeless, flat as a tapestry. Miss Moberly later wrote: "There were no effects of light and shade, and no wind stirred the trees. It was all intensely still." They continued along the path, however, and at length encountered two gardeners who were working with wheelbarrow and spade. The men were dressed in green, and on their heads they wore three-cornered hats. Miss Jourdain stopped to ask directions. One of the men pointed silently with his spade, and the women walked on.

They came upon a small cottage – or rather, Miss Jourdain recalled coming upon it and seeing this tableau: Two women stood framed in the doorway; one was handing a jug to the other. The women were wearing old-fashioned, full-skirted dresses; white handkerchiefs were draped around their necks and tucked into their bodices. Miss Moberly did not see this scene, and Miss Jourdain made no comment upon it at the time.

In a few moments more, the visitors realized that they were lost and became somewhat alarmed. Before them stood a little wood, surrounding a circular summerhouse that reminded Miss Moberly of a park bandstand. Both women saw the man who sat alone in the house, and both instinctively recoiled. He was dressed in a dark cloak and slouch hat. His face, too, was dark, and ugly with smallpox scars, and his expression was forbidding. The worst of this, however, was that he gazed directly at them yet seemed unaware of their presence. They were invisible to him.

Something was obviously amiss. The women turned in perplexity to each other. Just then, they heard running footsteps. The footsteps sounded behind them, but a young man suddenly appeared in front of them. He wore buckled shoes and a dark cloak of antique cut. "Mesdames," he hissed excitedly in French. "Don't go that way; go this way to find the house," and he pointed to the right. Having given these instructions, he smiled a curious smile, then turned and began to run. In another moment, he had vanished.

The Englishwomen followed his advice and took a path to the right. It carried them across a rustic bridge that spanned a narrow ravine. Within the ravine splashed a small waterfall, so close they could have touched it. The path brought them to a formal garden leading to a small, lovely house: They had arrived at the rear entrance of the Petit Trianon.

On the terrace, to one side of the graceful double staircase, Miss Moberly saw a woman in a white dress ornamented with a pale green fichu. The woman was sketching something with great intensity, but she looked up as they passed. Miss Moberly recalled later that she was pretty, if no longer young. Miss Jourdain did not see the woman; as before, she thought the place was deserted. She felt that there was something near, however, and then wondered why she felt so.

For both women, the perception of sadness and oppression had mounted to an almost intolerable level. It was relieved in short order by a young man, quite jaunty, who led them through the house and out the front door. With a mocking smile, he left them there. They found themselves in the middle of a chattering wedding party of French people. The feeling of oppression lifted at once; the breeze blew; the birds sang. As Miss Moberly later remarked, the Englishwomen felt quite lively again. Shortly thereafter, they took a carriage to the Hôtel des Réservoirs

in the village of Versailles and had tea.

Feeling relieved that the day was over, Miss Moberly and Miss Jourdain refrained from discussing their adventure. When they did at last, however, they agreed that they must have experienced a haunting. But what was it? Both of them set out to do some research, and they took care to write independent accounts of the episode.

In the course of their research, they discovered that other people had seen the hauntings at the Petit Trianon, and always in August. A second visit to Versailles revealed no bridge or ravine or waterfall or summerhouse. All of these had existed in 1789, but they had disappeared by 1901. The paths they had taken had disappeared as well. The door their jaunty guide had led them through had been blocked up for a century. They found that the gardeners of Versailles no longer wore the green uniforms that had been required in 1789.

Intelligent women that they were, they concluded with some reluctance that Versailles had presented them with its aspect on a certain day in 1789; and they knew the date, because a woman who had been there at the time had left behind an account of it—of Marie Antoinette, sketching in the sun and rising to greet the messenger running from Paris to tell her that a revolutionary mob was heading for Versailles. The evil-looking, dark-haired man was the Comte de Vaudreuil, lover of the Queen's closest companion and a star in the firmament when Marie Antoinette's court shone the brightest.

De Vaudreuil had encouraged the extravagant frivolities that helped to bring about the Queen's downfall, and he had benefited immensely from her generosity. When revolution was imminent, however, he fled Versailles—disguised, like other deserters among her coterie, for fear of the mob.

But the hauntings at the Petit Trianon always occurred in August, and the mob had come in October. Miss Moberly and Miss Jourdain advanced a theory for this discrepancy: They had seen their vision on August 10. On August 10, 1792, three years after the day in the garden at the Petit Trianon, the Royal Family was in Paris, running from sanctuary to sanctuary, always just a few steps ahead of the mob; it was on that date that Marie Antoinette realized that all was lost and that only her death would answer the anger of the people of France.

Perhaps, speculated the Englishwomen, Marie Antoinette in her agony had cast her thoughts back to those last moments in the sunlight on the pretty terrace, the moments before the messenger came to break her pleasant spell forever. Perhaps the intensity of the Queen's pain—and the imprint of a final moment upon the fabric of the house itself—had led to the haunting.

Who knew? By the time Marie Antoinette was guillotined in 1793, Versailles had been sacked; revolutionaries had stolen the gilded furniture from the grand chambers and effaced the royal motifs from the walls. But something of the spirit of the Petit Trianon survived. Why else would the house repeat its last bright moments for people who chanced there long years after? ༄

The perfect hiding place

Several English houses were haunted by spectral brides, but none more poignantly than Marwell Hall, near Owslebury in Hampshire. In this case, the bride suffered an appalling fate on her wedding day. Full of high spirits and still in her wedding finery, she insisted on a game of hide-and-seek with the guests. She was not found that day or the next or the next, although the whole countryside was searched. Finally, it became clear that she had died: Her ghost began to flit along the corridors and fumble at the locks.

Years later, the mystery was solved. A servant, exploring one of the many attics of the house, prized open an oak chest and found within a skeleton in bridal array. The bride had been too clever in her hiding place: Apparently the lid of the chest had fallen and locked. Now that it had at last been opened again, the hapless ghost was released from its torment and haunted Marwell Hall no more.

The Hooded Congregation

Amid the forested mountains of northern Sweden in centuries past, the long winter nights were crowded with the restless, greedy dead. The living, isolated for months in villages hidden among the fir trees, stayed indoors for the most part: They knew the darkness did not belong to them; they knew that things could happen outside the safe circle of the hearth that were best not risked or even thought of. This was especially true in the bleak time around the winter solstice, as a Christmas tale relates.

In her cottage on a hillside, a woman was awakened early one Christmas morning by church bells echoing in the air. When the peal ceased, she peered out the window. It was dark, as it would be until almost noon at that time of year, but far below she saw that the doors of the village church were thrown open and its light was streaming out in welcome. Although she could not be sure of the hour, it was clear that Christmas service was about to begin. In some haste, the woman dressed, wrapped herself in her warmest shawl, and taking a lantern to light her way, set out down the hill for the church.

None of her neighbors were in view, and nothing broke the enveloping silence except the occasional crackle of ice falling from tree branches and the crunching of the snow underfoot. As she neared the little church, however, she heard snatches of singing borne on the air, and she walked faster, spurred by the thought of warmth and companionship.

At the open church door, she set down her lantern and composed her thoughts to suit the joyful day. Within the nave were rows of hooded heads; her neighbors had been more alert than she, it seemed. Intoning psalms at the head of the congregation was a priest, robed not in the pristine white of this great festival but in indeterminate gray. He looked up at the woman peering into the church and bent once more to his prayers, so that his face was hidden.

She crept up the aisle between the rows of chanting worshippers, searching for a place to sit. Then help came: A gentle hand grasped her elbow and a soft voice spoke into her ear: "This way, dear one." Her rescuer guided her to the front of the church. The singers seated there shuffled sideways on their bench to make room, but such was their intentness on the hymn that not one looked up or greeted her. She sat down meekly, and her guide sat beside her.

Having settled herself in the pew, the woman turned to thank her helper. But the words died on her lips. The person sitting beside her had thrown back her concealing hood. The woman recognized the face at once, although it was much changed: It was the face of her beloved sister, whom she herself

had laid in her coffin that autumn, before the first snowfall.

The sister laid a bony hand upon the woman's arm, and the damaged face twisted into an expression that might have been pleading. It was hard to tell, for the head was little more than gleaming bone, still adorned with pasty shreds of flesh. The lipless mouth stretched open to speak, and a gust of odor— a sweet, necrotic scent tinged with the smell of earth—swept across the living visitor. No sound came from the mouth. But all around the woman eddied the almost toneless chanting of the clustered congregation.

She pulled her arm free from the bony clasp and began to inch across the bench. The figure gestured, and the woman found her voice. "You are the dead," she cried out sharply.

At once, as if a spell had been broken, the singing stopped, and a profound and listening silence settled upon the congregation. Heads turned toward her; hoods fell back. Shufflings and rustlings began, and whisperings without words.

The woman felt a hand on her shoulder and jerked around. Behind her was a gleaming skeleton and beside it another. All up and down the shadowy rows swayed the figures of the dead. Some, still partially clothed in flesh, she recognized: They were people from the village, or had been not long ago. Here a shoulder blade protruded from the rags of a dress; there, wisps of hair clung to a whitened skull. Some of the figures were no more than bone, and these she could not recognize. Some, no doubt dead longest, had faded to almost transparent shadows.

The congregation began to move, drifting in a blind and stumbling sort of way toward the living being among them, hands cupped to ears or outstretched, feeling the air. Her sister's voice sounded again close by. "They have heard you. Run, before they find you, for they will have you with them if they can: They hunger for fresh company."

And the woman rose trembling to her feet. She was as quiet as she could be, but each skull turned at once in her direction, and bony fingers pointed. She edged off the bench and stepped into the aisle. The ragged figures, clutching at one another, twittering and clicking their teeth, stretching their faces in gleaming grins, began to close in.

Stepping as lightly as she could, she hurried down the aisle, but they swarmed behind her, unerringly following the sound of her footsteps. She ran, smelling the earth smell and the stench of death, and at her back she felt sharp prodding. A hand grasped her shoulder; she shook it off. Fingers clutched at her shawl as she gained the door, and she slipped from the fabric and leaped out into the cold night air. Behind her, a single howl issued from the church, and that was all.

Gibbering with fear, she made for her priest's house, to find him just awake and preparing for Christmas Mass. After she told her tale, the priest himself, holding his crucifix high before him, led her back to the church.

The church was empty and peaceful. The shawl—or what little was left of it—lay near the door; it was torn and clawed almost beyond recognition.

Chapter Four

Hands across the Void

When Vikings ranged the northern seas, an island called Samsey off the coast of Jutland provided a haven for their long ships and, for some of the Scandinavian warriors, a final resting place. On the south shore of the island was a burial ground, a rocky heath dotted with funeral mounds. It was a lonely place, silent save for the deep breathing of the sea and the moan of the winter winds. Within the stone- and dirt-covered mounds, in chambers crowded with gilded daggers and heavy swords, fallen Vikings slept on, moldering in the dark. At night, flames— the mysterious "hovering fires" of the other world that shielded tombs from robbery—flickered over the mounds and upon the heath around them, and in the light of the fires moved the black and twisted shapes of barrow-wights, the restless dead who haunted burial sites.

Few of the living ever went to that heath—and those who did went only by day and to consign brave comrades to the earth. Once, however, a woman went there to seek out the dead.

She was an unusual woman for those times. Her name was Hervor, and she had been reared in the hall of her mother's father, a powerful jarl, or Norse chieftain, because her mother had no husband to care for the family. Fatherless, her heritage a mystery, Hervor grew up to be beautiful, but wild and combative. Disdaining the skirts of women and women's work at the loom and the embroidery frame, she dressed in the woolen trousers and tunic of a man. When she was old enough, she took to robbing wayfarers who crossed her grandfather's land. When he discovered this, he ordered her into women's clothes and had her sequestered in his hall, where the house slaves, whom Hervor mistreated as she did everyone around her, whispered that she was no more than a serf's bastard, the daughter of a swineherd who had seduced her mother.

But Hervor was a hero's daughter, and her grandfather told her so when she confronted him with the house slaves' gossip. Her father, said the old jarl, was Angantyr, one of the twelve sons of the great Viking Arngrim, all of whom had died in battle before Hervor's birth. Their burial mound was on the island of Samsey, and with them was buried Angantyr's invincible sword, which was named Tyrfing. A magic weapon made by dwarfs, the sword was a treasure to be claimed only by Angantyr's rightful heir.

Then Hervor left the hall to seek her inheritance from the father she had never known. She dressed again as a man and, taking a man's weapons, traveled alone until she met a band of Vikings. In their long ship, she sailed to Samsey.

The warriors she journeyed with refused to venture near the south side of the island. All of them knew that barrow-wights dealt savagely with anyone who would disturb the tombs. They were prepared to fight any living man, they said, but not to risk doing battle with the dead, even in the cause of a rightful claimant. Hervor argued with them for hours at the anchorage offshore, until at last they had her taken to the beach in a small boat. The oarsman left her there and sped back to the long ship, with never a glance at the island.

Dusk had already begun to settle over the heath, and the barrow fires were burning brightly. As Hervor crossed the harsh terrain, she met a lone shepherd who was gathering in his flock for the night. When she told him her mission, he stared and said that she was a fool to go to that place. The grave mounds were opening at this hour, he said, and deadly beings were abroad. He hobbled away with his sheep, and soon their anxious bleating and the dull clapping of their bells had faded out of hearing.

But the shepherd had said nothing about the burial place that Hervor did not already know, and so she went on, guided by the firelight. Soon enough, she was among the shadowed grave mounds, and tongues of flame sprang up on either side of her path. As she ad-

vanced into the field of the dead, she heard rumblings and rustlings; at the edges of her vision, black figures rose from the ground and moved in the flames, but when she turned to look at them directly, she saw only the fire. She had the sensation that something was stalking behind her, but again, when she turned, there was no sign of another presence among the mounds. Yet the feeling of deep malignity in the air intensified with every step she took.

At length Hervor came to a burial mound marked with a rune she recognized. She had found the funeral barrow of her father and his brothers.

Hervor stood before the entrance stone and examined its carvings. Presently, she cried, "Wake, Angantyr! Your daughter Hervor calls you."

The echo died and was not answered. All was quiet, except for the crackle of the barrow flames nearby — greenish flames that seemed to drain the color from the world and shed cold rather than heat.

Hervor called her father's name again and charged him to deliver the sword Tyrfing. Again, silence was her only reply.

She called a third time and bade her father answer, threatening him with a curse: "If you do not fetch the sword, may you feel maggots gnawing you forever as you molder." Moments passed, and then a voice spoke from within the mound, a muffled and chill voice with nothing in it of mortal mouth or throat or lungs.

"Why do you call me, Hervor? Daughter, you are mad to wake the dead." Around the stone, flames danced more brightly. Undaunted, Hervor again demanded her inheritance and added with the defiance of the young, "It does not become a ghost to bear costly arms."

There was a movement and a scraping noise at the tomb entrance then, and the dark line that defined the edge of the entrance stone grew wider. The stone had shifted, and a dank breath of air, heavy with the stench of decay, swept forth. Hervor flinched but stood her ground.

The cold voice spoke again, more clearly. It warned Hervor of the sword's power and of its poisoned edges. In ringing tones, it told the woman that no one would defeat her while she carried the sword but that Tyrfing would be the doom of her descendants. Hervor cared nothing for this and said so. She demanded her inheritance, as before.

The crack at the edge of the entrance stone widened suddenly. Something white flashed in the opening—an arm perhaps, although it moved too quickly for Hervor to be sure. An object whirled through the air, glinting. The sword Tyrfing, bright with silver filigree and glowing with jewels, clattered to the ground in front of her. She picked it up and sang a blessing over the tomb of her father. Then she walked back across the shadowed landscape to the world of the living.

Armed with her Tyrfing, Hervor grew calmer as she grew older. She married a powerful jarl and bore him two sons, and they were fierce warriors, as their grandfather had been. But the sword of the dead carried with it a curse. As Angantyr had foretold, the possession of it was the bane of Hervor's descendants, for their history was one of kin slaying.

Hervor's sons grew to be handsome, strong men; the elder, Angantyr, was good-hearted and well-loved, but the younger, Heidrek, had an evil nature. Heidrek murdered his brother at a feast— some say with a stone, others say with the sword Tyrfing. In any case, Heidrek was sent into exile for the crime, and he took the sword and its curse with him.

With the aid of the sword, Heidrek acquired power, lands and men enough to be called a King. He married the daughter of another King, a man who ruled great lands in Russia, and gained sole possession of the lands by killing his father-in-law. In her grief at this kin murder, Heidrek's wife hanged herself. Heidrek himself eventually died ignominiously at the hands of slaves he had captured in one of his many battles.

He left two sons, Hervor's grandchildren. One of them slew the other with Tyrfing in a dispute over the inheritance. After this deed, the cursed weapon vanished from history.

Hervor's tale is a complex one, but in its central event—the summoning of her father's spirit—it is far from unique. Throughout history (although far more often in the past than the present day), people have called the dead from their rest. Sometimes they did so inadvertently, releasing, through ignorance or carelessness, beings that should have been kept bound in their inimical world. But whether accidental or deliberate, such a disruption of the natural order of things was a serious business indeed.

Most people, of course, went to great pains to hurry the dead to their new home

In Denmark, ghosts that had been exorcised – forced down into the earth and pinned in place with a stake driven through the heart – did not rest easily. They lay in the dark, waiting for a chance to escape, and for that reason, people who ventured into lonely fields and meadows were warned not to disturb unmarked posts. Too often, those who touched the wood heard an eager, muffled voice demanding freedom from the post that held them down. "You pull," the voice would whisper, "and I will push."

Murder by spectral proxy

In Iceland, ghosts could be made by magic from a human bone. Called sendings, these ghosts were used as murderers, but they could be defeated. Once, for instance, there lived a handsome widow who was much sought after as a wife. She refused all her suitors, however, including one who was skilled in wizardry. After that proposal, the widow, a prescient woman, put herself on guard.

Her fears were realized one summer afternoon, when she was alone in her larder, preparing her farmhands' supper. All was still, but after a time, some sixth sense made her turn toward the door. She saw a shadow, as black and soft as smoke, save for a white spot in the center. It slid around the door and across the wall of the larder. She knew it for the wizard's sending.

When it came near, she struck with her knife at its one vulnerable place – the white spot. Instantly, knife and shadow vanished. In the morning, however, she found the knife in the yard; it was stuck through a splintered human bone. Bravery and a metal blade had done the trick, and the woman was disturbed no more.

and keep them in their place, and a range of funeral customs developed to ensure that they would not walk again.

In Britain, as soon as death occurred, doors and windows were opened to give easy passage to the departing soul, any knots in the house were loosened lest the spirit be caught in them, and mirrors were covered to keep the soul from being trapped in its own reflection. Domestic animals were put out of doors so that the new-freed soul would not enter one of them and haunt its master. Salt – in its purity an antidote to evil – often was placed on the corpse's breast.

Similarly, in Denmark the details of laying out the corpse were intended for the preservation of peace. The big toes were tied together to hobble the dead person; pennies were placed on the eyes to keep them shut, and open scissors were laid on the stomach because metal was believed to be a preventive of evil. Before the corpse was buried, nothing could move in a circular pattern in the house, since this was thought to disturb the dead; even the grinding of mustard and malt was forbidden, because of the rotation of the pestle during the grinding process.

In the days between death and burial, someone always watched beside the dead, and candles were set up around the body to keep back the encroaching dark. Tears were discouraged, and no tears were to fall on the face of the dead, because that made it more difficult for the soul to wrench itself away from those it had loved in life. The extreme of this behavior was to be found in the boisterous, all-night Irish wake, in which sorrow and fear were masked by laughter, song, drinking and even card playing.

When the body had been sealed in the prison of its coffin for burial, it was carried out of the house feet first, so the spirit might not easily trace back the route that led from home to cemetery. Sometimes coffins were carried round and round the burial ground, to perplex phantoms about the right way home.

The grave itself was provided from time immemorial with objects the dead one had cherished in life, so that ghosts would feel no need to walk among the living and retrieve their possessions. Viking graves such as Angantyr's were treasure hoards filled with warriors' weapons, their golden neck torques and arm rings, their gems, money and pottery, and the bodies of their slain horses. Sometimes, too, slaves were sacrificed and laid beside their masters and mistresses, to keep them company in the afterlife and prevent them from seeking companionship among the living.

Long after Europe left its barbarian days behind, the equipping of graves with worldly goods continued, but on a more modest scale. In many cases, objects that a person had nearby at the moment of death went into the grave, lest the person's spirit come seeking them after burial. The custom prevailed in every walk of life. Priests were buried with their sermons. Women who died in pregnancy received careful treatment, since they had need of materials for the child they might bear in the afterworld: They were buried with holy water to christen the baby, money to pay for the churching ceremony, swaddling clothes, and needle and thread.

Murderers, suicides and others who had violated the laws of society were meted rigorous attention after death because they were deemed more likely than their innocent fellows to menace the living. They therefore were buried at borderline locations—places that, being neither one thing nor another, were in a sense divorced from the defined world of the living. In Scandinavia, the graves of criminals often were sited at the borders of properties; the criminals' ghosts thus were trapped forever in a kind of territorial limbo. Witches and suicides were interred at crossroads, those quintessential in-between places.

Yet though the masses of humanity sought to give their dead decent burial and eternal sleep—to keep them in the other world and see them no more—there were always people like Hervor who called ghosts back from the grave. In the Nordic countries especially, ghosts were regularly summoned to render to the living the things that the living had need of—not only weapons but important buried objects such as books of magic. Nordic ghosts, notoriously cruel and murderous, might also be invoked to kill an enemy; such a ghost was called a sending, for it was sent by the living to perform a task that the living could not or would not do.

A more usual motive for raising the dead, however, was a kind of scholarly, power-seeking curiosity. Existing as they did in a world that was removed from the natural stream of time, ghosts could reveal the truths of any age, it was thought. People who dared to summon them might learn all of what was past or passing or to come. This was the principle behind necromancy, an ancient practice that literally means "divination by the dead."

The First Century Roman writer Lucan repeated a tale of an episode of necromancy in his *Bellum Civile*, which concerned the war between Julius Caesar and his rebellious general Gnaeus Pompeius Magnus—Pompey. With outraged disapproval, Lucan reported that Pompey's son Sextus Pompey devised a consultation with the dead shortly before he and his father engaged Caesar at Pharsalus in Thessaly in 48 B.C. Oracles, of course, were available to him, but these priestly seers often gave confusing responses to questions about the future, whereas—noted Lucan—"a man who dares consult the dead deserves to be told the truth."

The young Pompey engaged a witch called Erichtho to do his business, and she went to work in a rigidly organized fashion. She first obtained a fresh corpse to serve as a vessel for the spirit she would summon, endowing it with the power of speech. Older corpses in advanced stages of decay would not do: Sound lungs and a complete mouth and tongue were needed for clear speech. In the middle of the night, recounts Lucan, Erichtho anointed this corpse with an elixir of life, the least loathsome of whose ingredients were the sloughed skin of a snake and the froth of a rabid dog. Then, with incantations, the witch summoned a ghost—that of a soldier, because of Sextus Pompey's concern with warfare—to quicken the corpse and answer young Pompey's questions.

The result of her chants was astonishing. In Lucan's words, "The corpse's cold blood grew warm; it coursed into the blackened wounds and through each artery until it reached the fingers and toes. Both lungs began to work, and new life invaded the marrow of the bones, so that every joint throbbed, every muscle tightened, and then, instead of slowly raising itself limb by limb from the ground, it leaped up suddenly and stood erect. Granted, the jaw still hung down and the eyes glared; indeed, the corpse looked more like a dying man than one restored to life, because it remained pale and stiff and seemed stupefied by its return to the upper air. Nor did a sound come from the mouth; Erichtho's charm allowed the ghost to reply only, not to volunteer information."

Sextus Pompey wanted to know the outcome of the impending battle at Pharsalus; the ghost hinted that it would not be favorable to the Pompey faction. But it added, "Yours is an unlucky family; neither Europe nor Asia nor Africa can provide a refuge. Each of you will be buried in a different continent and all in countries over which your father has triumphed. The truth is that nowhere in the world will be much safer than Pharsalus."

With that the young Pompey had to be content. Because it was thought that death could not easily reclaim one who had been restored to life, Erichtho gave the corpse a second death: She burned it to ashes.

As for Sextus Pompey and his family, the ghost was right to be gloomy. Julius Caesar defeated them at Pharsalus. The elder Pompey fled to Egypt, parts of which he once had conquered, and was killed there. Sextus Pompey later died in Asia Minor and his elder brother, Gnaeus, in Spain, lands that their father had subdued in the days of his glory.

Lucan's account was well known in the Middle Ages and the Renaissance, when necromancy seems to have fascinated various wizards and scholars. Just how much they actually practiced this dark art is unclear, but they devoted a great deal of attention to its finer points, as diverse academic treatises and manuscripts show.

The general theory of summoning was simple: The summoner chose times and places propitious to disorder, since recalling the dead to life was a deliberate flouting of the rules of nature. Midnight was often recommended as suitable. Neither one day nor another, it is an in-between time when disorder might reign. And in-between places such as crossroads were favored for the same reason, although

Strange and perilous though it was, there were those among the living who sought to
raise the dead. With spells and incantations, these necromancers summoned
ghosts from the other world and forced the wraiths to do their bidding.

ghosts often were called in the very grave-yards where their bodies were buried.

For protection, the summoner surrounded himself with sanctity. The instructions for doing this varied, but the principles remained the same. The summoner drew a circle on the floor or ground; sometimes the circle enclosed a square or a pentacle. He inscribed the circle with the various names of God—God the Father, God the Son, God the Holy Ghost, Jehovah, Christ, Jesus, Father, Adonai, God of Gods, Light of Lights and so on. He also provided himself with a Bible, a crucifix and a vial of holy water. Thus defended, he stepped into the circle—now a purified and consecrated space—and called forth the dead. They would answer, but as long as the summoner remained within the circle, they could do him no harm, for they could not cross into sanctified space. When the summoner finished asking questions, he could dismiss the ghosts merely by ordering them in the name of God to retire—or so the books of magic said.

In truth, traffic with the dead was always a chancy business for the living, no matter what the protections. Any rent in the fabric of the world's proper order provided an entryway for inhabitants of the lands beyond the grave. Nevertheless, the risk was taken not only by necromancers but also by alchemists, physicians and others who worked with dead bodies to acquire a deeper knowledge of nature. In obtaining the bodies, however, the early scientists sometimes got more than they had bargained for. Events in a laboratory in Paris provide a case in point.

Several centuries ago, according to documents preserved by various French philosophical societies, an alchemist and physician acquired the body of an executed criminal in order to dissect it. With the help of his apprentice, he accomplished the grisly task and disposed of all the body parts except for some fragments of skull. These he ordered the apprentice to pulverize for use in a medical preparation, whose description has been lost. Then, since the hour was growing late, the physician left and headed for home.

The apprentice, who also served as the physician's night watchman in return for his room and board, was left alone among the flasks and crucibles that crowded the working chamber. He built up the fire to warm his hands and then perched himself on a stool at a table and went to work with mortar and pestle. Soon the skull was reduced to powdery fragments. The apprentice scooped them together and wrapped

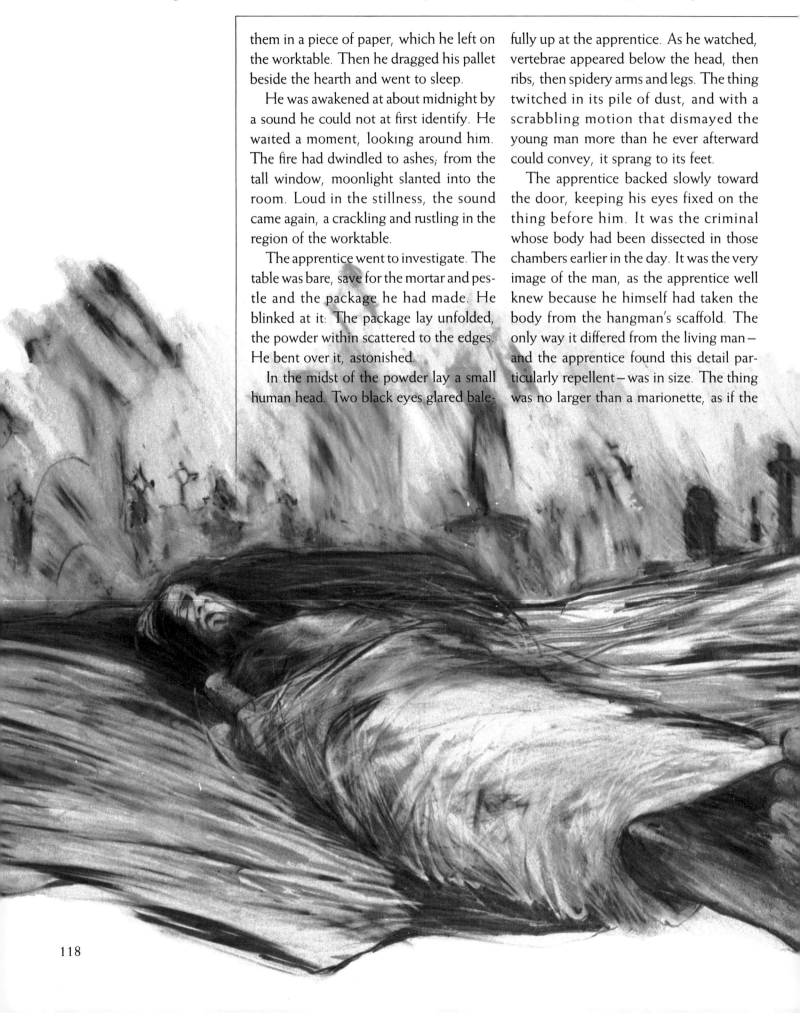

In a deed of singular scurrilousness, an Orkney Islands woman stole the embroidered winding sheet her neighbor had been buried in. Within a day, however, the dead woman appeared to fetch it back.

them in a piece of paper, which he left on the worktable. Then he dragged his pallet beside the hearth and went to sleep.

He was awakened at about midnight by a sound he could not at first identify. He waited a moment, looking around him. The fire had dwindled to ashes; from the tall window, moonlight slanted into the room. Loud in the stillness, the sound came again, a crackling and rustling in the region of the worktable.

The apprentice went to investigate. The table was bare, save for the mortar and pestle and the package he had made. He blinked at it: The package lay unfolded, the powder within scattered to the edges. He bent over it, astonished.

In the midst of the powder lay a small human head. Two black eyes glared bale-

fully up at the apprentice. As he watched, vertebrae appeared below the head, then ribs, then spidery arms and legs. The thing twitched in its pile of dust, and with a scrabbling motion that dismayed the young man more than he ever afterward could convey, it sprang to its feet.

The apprentice backed slowly toward the door, keeping his eyes fixed on the thing before him. It was the criminal whose body had been dissected in those chambers earlier in the day. It was the very image of the man, as the apprentice well knew because he himself had taken the body from the hangman's scaffold. The only way it differed from the living man — and the apprentice found this detail particularly repellent — was in size. The thing was no larger than a marionette, as if the

118

criminal's revenant had been diminished by the process of re-forming a whole body from the material of a skull.

It shook its tiny fist at him; it ground its teeth audibly. Then it crept to the edge of the table, shinnied down the leg to the floor, and sidled toward him, its shrill voice hissing incomprehensible imprecations. The apprentice cringed, but the dwarf creature did not harm him or even touch him. Still gibbering and muttering, it passed him, pushed open the door and vanished into the night.

Drenched with sweat and shivering with fear, the apprentice waited out the hours of darkness in his master's chambers, never taking his eyes from the door. The ghost of the criminal did not return, however.

Having retrieved what it could of its mortal remains, it retreated to whatever region claimed it and stayed there.

The lesson was clear enough, although it hardly needed to be taught anew: To interfere with the remains of mortality might disrupt the balance between this world and the one inhabited by the dead — with unpredictable consequences. Even tampering with objects that had been buried with the dead might stir up angry spirits. But the potential rewards of grave-robbing were great, and the reckless and greedy had risked ghostly wrath for treasure ever since humankind learned to bury its own. Thus, according to cuneiform chronicles al-

most three thousand years old, Assyrian plunderers sacked the royal tombs of the ancient civilization of Elam—and thereby "brought restlessness upon their ghosts." (The nature of that restlessness is unrecorded.) The tombs of the pharaohs were looted of their fabulous treasure, too, and few of the Viking hoards rested safe for all eternity. Even the graves of humble folk were robbed by the avaricious and foolish among the living.

One cautionary tale of such a deed comes from the wind-swept Orkney Islands, off the northern coast of Scotland. The hard-working fisherfolk who lived there were poor but proud. They took care that the dead were buried properly, in fine graveclothes and sturdy coffins. This particular tale concerns an old woman named Baubie Skithawa. She lived alone in a small stone cottage that was sparsely furnished but spotlessly clean: Not one of her neighbors could fault Baubie's well-scrubbed hearth or her pots and pans, hung in a shining row on the wall.

In a wooden chest, Baubie stored her linens, among them her own winding sheet. She had bought it at a fair and embellished it herself with rows of tatting on the edges and her name neatly picked out in satin stitch on one corner.

Baubie was frail and fading, but such was her concern for the proprieties that when she felt her time draw near, she called the village midwife—who also laid out the dead for burial—to inspect her graveclothes. The midwife thought them very fine and promised to do the old woman justice at her laying out.

Not long after the midwife's visit, Bau-bie did indeed die. Since she had no relatives, the midwife provided for her, opening the cottage doors and windows, putting out the cat and covering the mirror. Then she washed Baubie, wrapped her in her spotless winding sheet and laid the old woman out on the bed, as carefully as she had promised. When all was prepared, the midwife summoned the neighbors.

For two days and two nights, the men and women of the village kept a wake for Baubie Skithawa, sitting together in the little cottage, singing and praying and drinking brown ale. Among them was the Goodwife of Bae, familiarly known as Black Jock for her harsh ways and widely suspected of witchcraft. At intervals during the wake, Black Jock examined the pretty winding sheet with care and fingered the dainty edges.

"It's a pity to put such a fine cloth in the dirt," she said. No one replied, although their disapproval was clear enough from their expressions.

Except for that incident, the wake and the burial that followed were seemly. The neighbors dispersed to their own cottages, and Baubie Skithawa was left alone in her grave in the churchyard. But not for long, as it later was discovered. That very night, the Goodwife of Bae went to the churchyard and dug up the old woman's grave. It took her hours, but at last she reached the coffin, and from it she pulled the winding sheet, leaving the corpse pathetically naked. Then she filled in the grave again and went home to her cottage. She stored the winding sheet in her own linen chest.

The remainder of this tale was told by a man named Andrew Moodie, a neighbor of the Goodwife of Bae. Early in the evening of the day that followed the theft, Moodie, who was out on a simple errand, found himself trapped by a thunderstorm near the churchyard where Baubie lay. He took shelter under a tree, intending to wait out the rain. But fear shot through him as he looked toward the church.

Under rolling black clouds and lashing sheets of water, the graveyard was alight. From each stone rose a trembling, swaying pillar of fire, and in each glowing shaft a spirit writhed. Moodie recognized some of the faces. He saw his father. His mother beckoned him. And above the freshest grave he saw Baubie Skithawa, not soaring and dancing with her neighbors but huddled pitifully, trying to cover her nakedness. She alone was unclothed, and her neighbors, as censorious in death as they had been in life, pointed at her.

That was enough for Andrew Moodie. Averting his face to keep from meeting the ghosts' eyes—a sight that could strike a man senseless—he ran to the first cottage he saw and beat on the door.

Бe heard the scrape of metal within, and after an interminable pause, the door was opened a crack. The Goodwife of Bae, Black Jock herself, peered out. Stammering with fear, he begged for shelter. She hesitated a moment. Then, with a grunt, she let him in and bolted the door behind her.

She barred it, he noticed, with a wooden yoke used for carrying water pails, and he also noticed that metal awls—a protection against evil spirits—were stuck into the wood. The cottage was dark and stifling; the fire was out and rags were stuffed into the smoke hole in the roof, into the single deep window and even into the small opening under the eaves that the cat used as a doorway. The cat itself huddled by the cold hearth, ears back, growling.

Moodie opened his mouth to tell his tale, but the goodwife gave him an angry clout and bade him hold his tongue. She bent her head, listening, and Moodie, unnerved, listened too. He heard thunder and rain, and dimly underneath these sounds a wailing babble. This noise, a sound like the chattering of starlings, grew louder and closer. The door creaked and strained against its hinges. Then the rags fell from the window, the hole under the eaves and the smoke hole, and wind and water blasted into the cottage.

Panic-stricken, Moodie turned to the goodwife, but she was staring at the cathole under the eaves. A gray, rail-thin arm had pushed through the hole, and the bony fingers of its hand moved blindly in the air, clutching at nothing. The hand searched for a few moments more while Moodie and the Goodwife of Bae pressed themselves back against the wall farthest from it. Then it was withdrawn.

The goodwife groaned, and at that instant Moodie saw a face at the window and hands clutching the sill. The mouth in the face yawned in a gibbering howl, louder than the thunder, louder than the cacophony of voices eddying around the cottage. "Cold. Cold. Cold," it screamed. "Goodwife, I am clothed in cold."

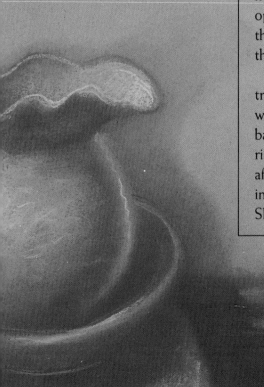

Emanations of grief could reach into the grave; sometimes, in fact, the dead were so disturbed by the weeping of their loved ones that they reappeared to demand peace.

Baubie Skithawa had come to reclaim her winding sheet.

That was almost the last thing Moodie remembered – groping arms and deafening screams. In the flickering glare of lightning flashes, he glimpsed the goodwife moving across the room to her linen chest; he saw a flash of white, and then he fainted.

He awoke in sunlight, roused by a cock's crow to a clear, bright, still morning. At the door were clustered his neighbors, anxiously whispering among themselves. Beside him, rigid with paralysis, lay the Goodwife of Bae, surrounded by rubble that once had been her possessions.

When Moodie at last was taken out of the cottage, he found that the woman's cows were dead in the byre and her garden torn to pieces. But the churchyard down the lane was dreamily peaceful, its grass smooth, its tombstones whitewashed. The grave of Baubie Skithawa, still mounded with fresh dirt, appeared to be undisturbed. And so it remained ever after. The old woman was at rest, having retrieved from the living what was her own.

The interruption of Baubie Skithawa's sleep had been caused by action that was not only deliberate but malicious. At the opposite extreme of summonings were those caused – always unintentionally – by the grief of the living.

A demonstration of the power of distraught love was provided by a Danish woman named Eliza, whose young husband died within a few days of their marriage. Her grief was devastating. Night after night she sat alone in her chamber in the dark, disdaining even candlelight. She contemplated the empty years that stretched ahead and wept without cease.

One night, however, she was interrupted by a tapping on the window. She called out; the voice that answered was her husband's. At once Eliza threw back the bolt and opened her door.

She was assailed by the scent of earth. With tear-clouded eyes, she peered into the shadows of the hall, and there she saw her husband. He was as tall as he had been in life, but gaunt and white, with sunken eyes that stared fixedly at her. On his back, he bore his coffin. He said nothing, but when Eliza stepped back he glided into the room.

He knelt before her, and she stroked his head. Her tears coursed down her face and fell onto his hair, and at last he spoke. It was her weeping that had wrested him from his grave. He told her about his long hours in the tomb; he said that he had no repose there, for each time her tears fell, blood filled his coffin. He begged her to cease her weeping and let him rest.

They sat quietly together through the night, and when the first hint of light appeared in the sky, the ghost rose and shouldered his coffin once more. Ghosts, he said, could not walk after daybreak. Unable to bear the parting, Eliza followed him through the house, out through the garden and down the familiar path to the graveyard. There she saw him grow even paler, slip into his coffin and, locked within it, slide into the earth.

She wept no more but she fell into a numb and trancelike state, as if her heart

had turned to ice. Within days she died and joined her bridegroom.

Because the weeping that had roused him ceased, the ghost of Eliza's husband never walked again. Generally, ghosts—whether haunting of their own volition or called by the living—retreated to their silent realm when the disturbance that had troubled them came to an end, or an imbalance between the worlds of the living and the dead was set right, or an incomplete task was finished. Thus, for instance, ghosts who haunted because they had a sin to confess or a message to convey retired when their confessions had been made or their tales had been told. The ghost of Dorothy Dinglet, for example, rested only after she had confessed a sin to curate John Rudall.

Similarly, the ghosts of children who had died unbaptized could be given peace by the bestowal of the name they lacked. It was thought in Britain that kindly people who saw these pathetic little spirits could ease their pain by dousing them with water and reciting the formula, "I baptize thee in the name of the Father, the Son and the Holy Ghost," then naming them John or Joan. But sometimes the process was less orderly than that:

Two centuries ago, it is said, the Scottish village of Whittinghame was haunted by the ghost of a child who had been killed by its mother. It harmed no one, but it could be seen each night, a flicker of white that ran restlessly from tree to tree in the churchyard. Its reedy, keening wails echoed through the village, tug-ging powerfully at all who heard. But no one would go near the churchyard at night, much less dream of responding to the ghost's unhappy cries. People in those parts believed that speaking to a ghost brought death to the speaker.

Late one evening, however, a drunken villager, staggering home from the ale-house, saw the little creature. He peered over the churchyard wall to watch it and then, with reeling bonhomie, spoke to it.

"How is it with ye, Short Hoggers?" he shouted. "Short hoggers" was a phrase that meant "baby booties." It was an affectionate tag often used in addressing small children, but it clearly was name enough for the ghost. The man heard its tinkling laugh and saw it clap its hands; then he saw it no more, and neither did anyone else in the village. Having been given a name, it had gone to its rest.

But such simple methods of sending ghosts away did not always work. Ghosts impelled by hatred of the living required sterner dismissals. In those cases, the courage and will of the living had to be pitted against the determination of the dead, and the rituals of exorcism came into play. In the Scandinavian countryside, this rite once was known as *at mane ned*, or "forcing down." To rid a place of haunting, priests or wise folk of peculiar power would, by the force of will and incantation, compel ghosts to sink into the ground. If the will of the exorcist was strong enough, the ghost could be driven far from human habitation and forced down there; very powerful ghosts, however, might well be forced down in the very places they haunted—in a vicarage garden,

Confession from beyond the grave

On a night in January of 1665, a Cornish clergyman conducted a successful exorcism in a field in the parish of South Petherwin. The ghost he exorcised was that of Dorothy Dinglet, a spinster whose spirit had repeatedly frightened a child of the neighborhood by appearing in the field (*page 28*). The clergyman, John Rudall, had seen her himself and, being a kind man, sought to give her peace.

First he measured a circle on the ground, marked a pentacle within it and set there a bunch of rowan boughs – rowan being a protection against evil. Then, with prayers, he summoned Dorothy Dinglet, who appeared with a "soft and rippling sound," he later wrote. In a variant of the usual practice, Rudall ordered the ghost into the circle. Normally, the summoner occupied the circle; Rudall never explained his deviation – but it worked: The spirit obligingly drifted to the center of the ring.

Rudall charged Dorothy Dinglet to tell him the reason she could not rest. She replied at once: She had sinned, she said, and gave Rudall the man's name, telling him never to reveal it. Then she disappeared.

The following morning at dawn, Rudall called forth the ghost again. Once more she floated into the field, and Rudall spoke to her, reporting that he had talked all night with the man in the case, who had expressed great remorse and promised to do penance. The wraith listened gravely to this intelligence and said nothing. When Rudall ordered her to depart, however, she sighed, "Peace be in our midst," and drifted away in a westerly direction, never to be seen again.

125

A careless word could call a ghost, as happened at a 17th Century trial in Cornwall. The dishonest defendant invoked as his witness a dead man, Jan Tregeagle. To his dismay, Tregeagle's spirit instantly appeared and refuted his story.

for instance, or in the cellar of a house. Once this had occurred, the ghosts, which in those times had a corporeal as well as a spiritual dimension, were held in place by stakes driven through their hearts.

In more sophisticated societies, the Church provided an elaborate exorcism ceremony that included adjurations, prayers, creeds and psalms, carefully recorded in appendixes to the written rituals of religion. Ghosts were servants of Satan, it was said, and thus the exorcising priests addressed the spirits in Satan's name: "I adjure you, ancient serpent," the priest chanted, "by your Creator and the Creator of the world, by Him who has power to send you to hell. Depart immediately with fear and with your army of terror."

This practice was frequently effective, but exorcists sometimes deviated from the prescribed form. Very malevolent ghosts might not be sent away into the dark; instead, the exorcism was used to bind the ghosts on earth and render them harmless to the living.

During the 17th Century, this occurred in Cornwall, in a place haunted by a ghost who had been inadvertently called from the grave. His name was Jan Tregeagle, and though the stories about him conflict, he seems to have been a magistrate in the town of Trevorder, near the bog-pitted, boulder-littered waste of Bodmin Moor.

Tregeagle was the very last person anyone would want back from the dead. In life he had been a tyrannical and dishonest judge, easily bribed, and a cruel and rapacious landlord. It was also whispered that he had seduced and murdered his own sister and tortured his wife and children to death. He was immensely wealthy, however, and very clever. He never was prosecuted in life and, fearing the punishments of hell after death, he bribed the priests of his parish to bury him in consecrated ground—a place quite unsuitable for one so unremittingly, squalidly evil.

Tregeagle died and was buried, and the people in the villages bordering Bodmin Moor breathed more easily. But he rose from the dead, and all because of one man's careless tongue.

Some months after his death, a legal dispute arose between a moneylender and his debtor, both of whom had been involved—to their shame—with Tregeagle. The case dragged on for weeks, ranging through a maze of shabby dealings, but the center of the argument—the matter of the moneylender's loan, which had not been repaid—was finally reached on a summer afternoon in a courtroom where the Bodmin Assizes were held.

It was quite hot and very still in the room. The lawyers, perspiring in ruffles and waistcoats and woolen stockings, were reduced to snarling arguments. Glassy-eyed with boredom, the judge stared out the window at a green lawn and shady trees and thought of sea breezes. The debtor in the case stubbornly refused to admit, even under the sternest examination, that he had had a contract with the moneylender or that he had borrowed money.

The moneylender's lawyer pointed out that there had been a witness to the transaction and that the witness was Jan Tregeagle. The debtor's lawyer replied with a sour smile that Tregeagle, being dead, could be of little use in the matter. At this point the debtor lost his temper. He denied once more that he had borrowed money – a lie, as it turned out – and he added an oath for which he was to be very sorry indeed: "If Tregeagle ever saw it, I wish to God he would come and declare it!" he snapped.

In the instant of silence that followed that proclamation, the floor of the courtroom seemed to shift. Then the door swung open to reveal the figure of Jan Tregeagle, dressed in seemly fashion in his graveclothes – the robes and bands of his magisterial office. His face, however, was far from seemly: It was as dark as earth and pitted with decay, and its black, lashless eyes glittered maniacally. It commanded the absolute attention of the lawyers, the moneylender, the debtor and even of the judge, who withdrew his gaze from the window and stared open-mouthed.

The ghost's message was brief. "He owes the sum," said Tregeagle, nodding at the debtor. Then he trod noiselessly to the debtor's side and hissed in his ear, "You will not find it so easy to be rid of me as it was to call me."

This proved to be the case. The debtor paid the moneylender, but he was a haunted man after that. When he climbed the stairs to bed at night, he heard shuffling in the shadows; when he lay in bed, the bed curtains shifted rhythmically, as if a hand were groping for the opening. Sometimes in daylight he caught a glimpse of the magistrate's gown, draped on the floor at the edge of a church pew or flicking out from behind a door. Sometimes he saw the ghost itself, beckoning with its ivory hand.

It continually cast nervous glances over its shoulder, and the debtor could see why. Tregeagle was pursued by a band of black and shapeless shadows. Once out of consecrated ground, the ghost was unprotected against the demonic agents of hell.

After some days of this, the debtor grew desperate. Haggard as the ghost itself, he went to his parish priest and begged for relief. Behind the priest's shoulder as he talked, the ghost of Tregeagle twitched and nodded madly.

Although the tales of what happened after this incident differ, most agree that the priest used the powers vested in him to exorcise the ghost. But the churchman hesitated to send Tregeagle back into the dark and sacrifice a soul to hell. Instead, he bound the magistrate with oaths and set Tregeagle to work at an endless task in a locale far removed from the dwellings of the living. The priest forced Tregeagle to a place known as Dozmary Pool, a vast and lonely sheet of water bordered by rushes and seldom visited by the Cornish. The task given was to empty the pool, which was thought to be bottomless.

It was said by those who ventured near at night that Tregeagle could be seen in the moonlight, at the edge of the pool, a bent figure ceaselessly scooping up water with the aid of a small limpet shell, just as the priest had ordered. Winds swept across the pool, rain beat upon it, ice covered it and had to be broken, and still the ghost performed its never-ending work.

This went on for years, and the debtor

and the villagers of the area were left undisturbed. One night, however, hideous howling was heard far out on Bodmin Moor; the next night, it came nearer; and the third night, the townsfolk of Trevorder heard it in their streets. Tregeagle — evil haunter, himself haunted by evil demons — was back, and there would be no peace for the living.

The priest was called in again; and again, with bell, book and candle, with somber oaths and earnest adjurations, he bound the ghost.

Some tales say that Tregeagle was made to spin ropes from sand at a place on the north coast of Cornwall, and that his desolate wailing could be heard each night as the wind and tide washed his work away. Some say that he was forced to carry sacks of sand across a stretch of the south coast, clearing one beach to make another. But according to most stories, the priest sent the magistrate to Land's End and bade him carry sand from Porthcurno Cove around a high and rocky headland to Nanjisal Cove. What with the difficulty of negotiating the granite cliffs and the sweep of wind and wave, this job was truly endless. Tregeagle and his demon followers never menaced the living again.

The Cornish said, however, that at Land's End, the long moaning of the sea winds was the sobbing of Jan Tregeagle, and that the howling of the North Atlantic storms revealed him raging still. Those who wanted to know what a ghost sounds like had only to venture to the Land's End cliffs and hear Tregeagle bemoaning the fate that bound him for all eternity.

But Tregeagle's cries were heard less often as the years passed. The stories of his misdeeds and of his hauntings grew garbled. Sometimes he was confused with other malefactors, so that the real Tregeagle became a being hard to discover. The images of his evil doings and of his sufferings after death grew thin and transparent, nothing more than ghosts of a ghost. In the end, the real tale dwindled to a trivial story used to frighten naughty children.

And this was true of many ghosts; as the world grew crowded with the heedless living, the powers of the dead began to fail. Out of haunted houses, away from the mortal world, streamed the restless spirits of the dead, driven away as much by inattention as anything else.

"Do you believe in ghosts?" an 18th Century French courtier once asked that witty woman of letters, the Marquise du Deffand.

"Oh, no," she replied. "But I am afraid of them."

Although she subscribed to the rationality of an enlightened age, the countess had not forgotten that even the most ordered human life was no more than a brief passage from darkness to darkness, a bright interval in a lightless eternity peopled with howling horrors.

And her approach is eminently sensible in any age. Those who lie alone do well to remember the eternal darkness when they hear footsteps in an upstairs hallway or shufflings on the stair, or see the curtains stirring when no breeze blows, or watch shadows shape themselves in dusky corners near the bed.

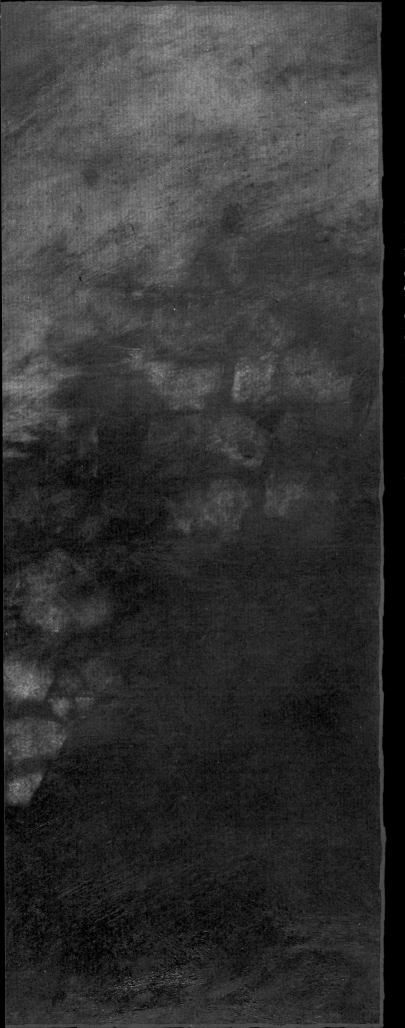

Glam's Tale

In days gone by, the barren mountains and bleak, rock-strewn pastures of Iceland were roamed by cruel ghosts, enemies of all who lived. Called "walkers after death," they were animated corpses, horrible to behold and perilous to encounter. The walkers were most active during the long winter nights; indeed, their presence sometimes grew so unbearable that the living made attempts to fight them. The story of Glam tells of such a battle:

Glam, a man with hair like wolf's fur and staring gray eyes, was a shepherd for a farmer named Thorhall, whose pastures lay in the north of the island. He was surly and violent by nature, and his lonely calling suited him. He met a lonely end: At the farmstead one night, he flew into a fury over some inconsequential matter, strode into a snowstorm, and he did not return.

When the blizzard abated the next day, the shepherd's black and bloated corpse was found in a valley not far away. It was surrounded by bloody footprints, and the farmers muttered that Glam had fought a walker. Shivering in the wind, they piled stones around the body to make a barrow, then trudged home. It could not be said that they mourned him, but they pitied anyone who suffered such a fate.

The burial was followed by fearsome events. That night, Thorhall's horses leaped screaming from their stalls, pursued by something that no one saw. In the morning, the animals were dead, their bones crushed, their flesh torn.

Next, howlings began. Through the winter nights, hoarse wailing raged around the farmhouse, while Thorhall and his family huddled within. And that was not all. Sometimes the roof beam sagged above them and heels drummed on the eaves; dampness ran down the shaking walls

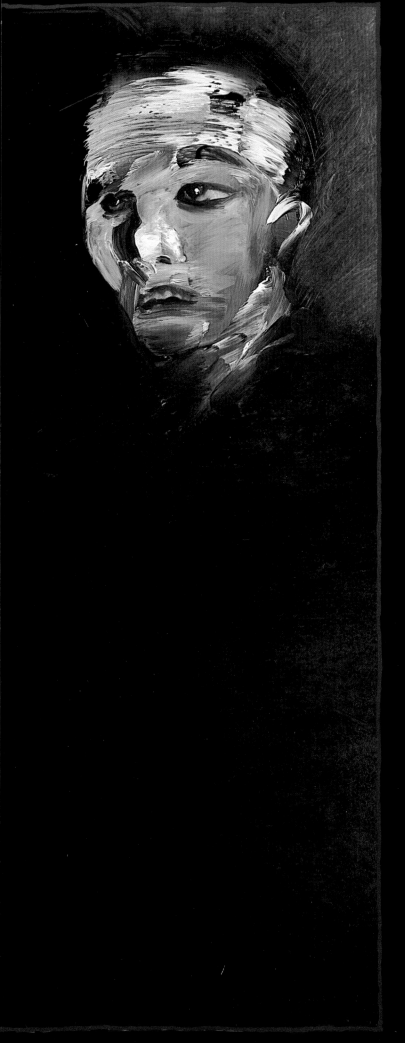

of the house and gathered in dismal puddles on the floors. On other nights, something clawed and scrabbled at the door, or in the moonlight outside, a hulking shadow shambled crazily to and fro, shaking a thatch of wolf-dark hair. Finally Thorhall realized that what was left of Glam's body had been invaded by the walker that killed him. A siege of the living had begun.

Daylight allowed the family some peace, but winter days in that northern land are short, and Glam returned as soon as darkness fell. The creature was not content with assaulting the house or lurking outside. In the outbuildings and pastures, it killed all that lived. Defeated, Thorhall fled with his family, leaving the farm to Glam.

Summer arrived at last, with its sunlit Arctic night, and then the farm was quiet again and Thorhall reclaimed it. But Glam's power revived as the days drew in. The ghost's autumn ragings were as deadly as before.

Word of the haunting reached the ears of a champion called Grettir the Strong, who journeyed to Thorhall's farm to battle the ghost of Glam. A night came when Grettir waited alone in the hall of the farmhouse, concealed in the folds of a furred cloak.

Hours passed quietly. Then, without even the rustle of a breeze to break the silence, a shadow slid into the room. It was followed by a livid face that turned blindly from side to side, scenting new blood. Grettir made no move.

The thing he saw in that hall had the shape of a man, but it smelled of rotten flesh and walked in an awkward, lumbering way, as if the spirit within was unfamiliar with the patterns of human movement. It made unerringly for the furred cloak, however, and its great hands clawed and tugged the fabric. Grettir set his feet against a

135

loose floor plank. Glam pulled again, so hard that the cloak and the man wearing it sprng up against the ghost's massive body. The clk fell away and Grettir stood revealed. He jerked himself free of the grip of the ghost and began to circle it, looking for an opening or advantage. The ghost's great head swung from side to side, following Grettir's movement.

Then mortal and spirit lunged at each other simultaneously, pitting strength against strength. Grettir was a mighty wrestler, so confident of his abilities that he left his dagger sheathed even in this deadly battle. The pair struggled in silence, save for Grettir's harsh breathing and the creak and thud of bodies slamming against the house posts and into the walls. Each step Glam took was toward the door. The spirit's strength increased in the cold night air. Every move Grettir made was to keep the battle in the house, within the walls of the living.

Back and forth they lurched and tumbled, and the fight began to go to Glam. Slowly the ghost wrestled the man to the door. It towered there at the border of its world, its back to the air and its relentless hands pulled Grettir into its embrace. Grettir stood like a pillar, feet braced against the threshold stone, hands against the frame.

The fighters swayed thus for moments more, while the mortal's strength ebbed and the ghost's grew. Then Grettir tried his last hope. He released his grip on the doorframe and lunged forward into Glam's straining arms. The ghost was overbalanced and fell backward to the ground just by the door. Grettir sprang up at once, but the creature lay still, flat on its back, its white, blank eyes staring up at the moon.

The sight of those eyes drove the strength from Grettir. Unable to draw his dagger, he stood

M. ARisman

helpless by the ghost of Glam. But the creature was defeated by the fall at the man's hands. It rose to a sitting position in the doorway and spoke in harsh, clicking tones. It said that Grettir would be friendless for the rest of his life and that he would see always through the eyes of Glam.

To stop the voice, Grettir struck. His dagger glittered in the moonlight; a gaping wound opened in the ghost's white throat. His hand gripping the leathery neck, Grettir called for Thorhall, who crept from the place where he had hidden during the fight. Thorhall stared while Grettir cut off the head.

Together, the men burned the body, and when it was reduced to ash and the last acrid smoke had drifted away, they buried the fragments in a spot where neither human nor beast would be likely to venture. Glam never tormented Thorhall again.

As for Grettir, he took his leave, much thanked by the farmer. But Grettir was a changed man, for he had absorbed something of the ghost, as the ghost had said he would. His temper grew short and his manner sullen. He fought with other men and hated their company; he was as impatiently evil-tempered as Glam had been in his shepherd's life. Yet Grettir feared to be alone. He saw more than his companions saw, especially in the dark, and the things he saw were foul, gibbering phantoms, always around him, always reaching for his hand. He saw, people said, with ghost's sight. Unfit to live with anyone, unable to live by himself, terrified of the dark, he passed his few remaining years in misery and died despised. In the end, thus, the ghost was the victor.

Bibliography

Alexander, Marc, *British Folklore*. New York: Crescent Books, 1982.

Ariès, Philippe, *The Hour of Our Death*. Transl. by Helen Weaver. New York: Vintage Books, 1982.

Barrett, Francis, *The Magus*. Secaucus, New Jersey: The Citadel Press, 1980.

Benneville, James S. de, transl., *The Yotsuya Kwaidan, or O'Iwa Inari*. Philadelphia: J. B. Lippincott, 1917.

Borrow, George, transl., *Romantic Ballads*. Norwich, England: Jarrold and Sons, 1913.

Briggs, Julia, *Night Visitors: The Rise and Fall of the English Ghost Story*. London: Faber and Faber, 1977.

Briggs, Katharine:

Abbey Lubbers, Banshees & Boggarts: An Illustrated Encyclopedia of Fairies. New York: Pantheon Books, 1979.

British Folktales. New York: Pantheon Books, 1977.

A Dictionary of British Folk-Tales in the English Language. London: Routledge & Kegan Paul, 1971.*

An Encyclopedia of Fairies. New York: Pantheon Books, 1976.*

Bringsværd, Tor Age, *Phantoms and Fairies from Norwegian Folklore*. Transl. by Pat Shaw Iversen. Oslo: Johan Grundt Tanum Forlag, no date.

Canning, John, ed., *50 Great Ghost Stories*. New York: Bell Publishing, 1971.

Cavendish, Richard, *The Black Arts*. New York: G. P. Putnam's Sons, 1967.

Cavendish, Richard, ed., *Man, Myth & Magic*. 11 vols. New York: Marshall Cavendish, 1983.*

Christiansen, Reidar, ed., *Folktales of Norway*. Transl. by Pat Shaw Iversen. The University of Chicago Press, 1964.

Craigie, William A., ed. and transl., *Scandinavian Folk-Lore*. Detroit: Singing Tree Press, 1970 (reprint of 1896 edition).

Crowe, Catherine, *The Night Side of Nature, or Ghosts and Ghost Seers*. London: George Routledge and Sons, 1866.

Cutt, Nancy and W. Towrie, *The Hogboon of Hell, and Other Strange Orkney Tales*. London: André Deutsch, 1979.

Daniels, Cora Linn, and C. M. Stevans, eds., *Encyclopaedia of Superstitions, Folklore, and the Occult Sciences of the World*. Vol. 1. Detroit: Gale Research, 1971 (reprint of 1903 edition).*

Davidson, Hilda R. Ellis, and W. M. S. Russell, eds., *The Folklore of Ghosts*. Cambridge, England: D. S. Brewer for the Folklore Society, 1981.*

Deane, Tony, and Tony Shaw, *The Folklore of Cornwall*. Totowa, New Jersey: Rowman and Littlefield, 1975.

De Givry, Grillot, *Witchcraft, Magic & Alchemy*. Transl. by J. Courtenay Locke. New York: Dover Publications, 1971 (reprint of 1931 edition).

De Tuddo, Italo, *Maldiroma*. Rome: Ner, 1981.

Evans-Wentz, W. Y., *The Fairy-Faith in Celtic Countries*. Secaucus, New Jersey: University Books, 1966.

Folklore, Myths and Legends of Britain. London: The Reader's Digest Association, 1973.

Graves, Robert, ed., *English and Scottish Ballads*. London: Heinemann, 1969.

Haining, Peter, *The Leprechaun's Kingdom*. New York: Harmony Books, 1980.

Halford, Aubrey S. and Giovanna M., *The Kabuki Handbook*. Rutland, Vermont: Charles E. Tuttle, 1956.

Harper, Charles G., *Haunted Houses*. Detroit: Tower Books, 1971 (reprint).*

Henderson, William, *Notes on the Folklore of the Northern Counties of England and the Borders*. Totowa,

New Jersey: Rowman and Littlefield, 1973 (reprint of 1866 edition).

Hight, George Ainslie, transl., *The Saga of Grettir the Strong: A Story of the Eleventh Century*. London: J. M. Dent & Sons, 1929.

Hole, Christina, *Haunted England: A Survey of English Ghost-Lore*. New York: Charles Scribner's Sons, 1941.*

Hunt, Robert, ed., *Popular Romances of the West of England*. New York: Benjamin Blom, 1968 (reprint of 1916 edition).

Johnson, W. Branch, *Folktales of Brittany*. London: Methuen & Company, 1927.

Killip, Margaret, *The Folklore of the Isle of Man*. London: B. T. Batsford, 1975.

Lang, Andrew, *The Book of Dreams and Ghosts*. New York: Ams Press, 1970 (reprint of 1897 edition).

Leach, Maria, ed., *Funk & Wagnalls Standard Dictionary of Folklore, Mythology and Legend*. 2 vols. New York: Funk & Wagnalls, 1949.*

Leiter, Samuel L., transl., *Kabuki Encyclopedia*. Westport, Connecticut: Greenwood Press, 1979.

Lindow, John, *Swedish Legends and Folktales*. Berkeley: University of California Press, 1978.

Lucanus, Marcus Annaeus, *Pharsalia: Dramatic Episodes of the Civil Wars*. Transl. by Robert Graves. Baltimore: Penguin Books, 1957.

Macaulay, Thomas Babington, *The History of England from the Accession of James II*. Vol. 3. New York: Lovell, Coryell, no date.

MacCulloch, John Arnott, *The Mythology of All Races*, Vol. 2, *Eddic*. New York: Cooper Square, 1964.*

MacCulloch, John Arnott, and Jan Machal, *The Mythology of All Races*, Vol. 3, *Celtic, Slavic*. New York: Cooper Square, 1964.*

MacGregor, Alasdair Alpin, *The Peat-Fire Flame: Folk-Tales and Traditions of the Highlands & Islands*. Edinburgh: The Moray Press, 1937.

Maple, Eric, *The Realm of Ghosts.* New York: A. S. Barnes, 1964.*

Marshall, Sybil, *Everyman's Book of English Folktales.* London: J. M. Dent & Sons, 1981.

Maugham, W. Somerset, *Sheppey: A Play in Three Acts.* London: William Heinemann, 1933.

Norton-Taylor, Duncan, *The Celts* (The Emergence of Man series). New York: Time-Life Books, 1974.

O'Donnell, Elliott:
Scottish Ghost Stories. Norwich, England: Jarrold Colour Publications, 1981 (reprint).
The Screaming Skulls and Other Ghost Stories. New York: Taplinger Publishing, 1969.

Palmer, Roy, *The Folklore of Warwickshire.* Totowa, New Jersey: Rowman and Littlefield, 1976.

Piper, David, *The Companion Guide to London.* London: Collins, 1968.

Porter, Enid, *The Folklore of East Anglia.* Totowa, New Jersey: Rowman and Littlefield, 1974.

Price, Harry, *Poltergeist over England: Three Centuries of Mischievous Ghosts.* London: Country Life, 1945.

Raven, Jon, *The Folklore of Staffordshire.* Totowa, New Jersey: Rowman and Littlefield, 1978.

Robbins, Rossell Hope, *The Encyclopedia of Witchcraft and Demonology.* New York: Crown Publishers, 1959.

Scott, A. F., *Witch, Spirit, Devil.* London: White Lion Publishers, no date.

Shakespeare, William, *Shakespeare, Complete Works.* Ed. by W. J. Craig. Oxford University Press, 1980.

Simpson, Jacqueline, *Icelandic Folktales and Legends.* Berkeley: University of California Press, 1979.*

Smith, Goldwin, *A History of England,* 4th ed. New York: Charles Scribner's Sons, 1974.

Spence, Lewis:
British Fairy Origins. Wellingborough, Northamptonshire, England: The Aquarian Press, 1981.
The Fairy Tradition in Britain. London: Rider and Company, 1948.

Squire, Charles, *Celtic Myth & Legend, Poetry & Romance.* North Hollywood, California: Newcastle Publishing, 1975.

Thiselton-Dyer, T. F., *The Ghost World.* London: Ward & Downey, 1893.

Thompson, C. J. S., *The Mystery and Lore of Apparitions.* London: Harold Shaylor, 1930.

Thompson, Stith, *Motif-Index of Folk-Literature.* Vol. 2. Bloomington: Indiana University Press, 1955.*

Thorpe, Benjamin, comp., *Northern Mythology.* 3 vols. London: Edward Lumley, 1852.

Tolkien, Christopher, transl., *The Saga of King Heidrek the Wise.* London: Thomas Nelson and Sons, 1960.

Tryckare, Tre, *The Viking.* Gothenburg, Sweden: Cagner & Co., 1966.

Tuchman, Barbara W., *A Distant Mirror. The Calamitous 14th Century.* New York: Alfred A. Knopf, 1978.

Underwood, Peter, *A Gazetteer of Scottish and Irish Ghosts.* London: Souvenir Press, 1973.

Whitlock, Ralph:
The Folklore of Devon. Totowa, New Jersey: Rowman and Littlefield, 1977.
The Folkore of Wiltshire. London: B. T. Batsford, 1976.

Ziegler, Philip, *The Black Death.* New York: Harper & Row, 1971.

Titles marked with an asterisk were especially helpful in the preparation of this volume.

Acknowledgments

The editors are particularly indebted to John Dorst, consultant, for his help in the preparation of this volume.

The editors also wish to thank the following persons and institutions: Lucio Anzalone, Rome; François Avril, Curator, Département des Manuscrits, Bibliothèque Nationale, Paris; Françoise Belin, Musée des Beaux-Arts, Nantes; Elena Bradunas, American Folklife Center, Library of Congress, Washington, D.C.; Ann Kuhns Corson, Alexandria, Virginia; Geneviève Deblock, Bibliothèque de l'École Nationale Supérieure des Beaux-Arts, Paris; Clark Evans, Rare Book and Special Collections Division, Library of Congress, Washington, D.C.; Marielise Göpel, Archiv für Kunst und Geschichte, West Berlin; Gustav Henningsen, Archivist, Danish Folklore Archives, Copenhagen; Christine Hoffmann, Bayerische Staatsgemäldesammlungen, Munich; Heidi Klein, Bildarchiv Preussischer Kulturbesitz, West Berlin; Kunsthistorisches Institut, Universität, Bonn; B. W. Robinson, London; Justin Schiller, New York City; Robert Shields, Rare Book and Special Collections Division, Library of Congress, Washington, D.C.; Claude Souviron, Curator, Musée des Beaux-Arts, Nantes; A. H. Wesencraft, Harry Price Collection, University of London Library.

Picture Credits

The sources for the illustrations in this book are shown below. When known, the artist's name precedes the picture source.

Cover: Horace Vernet, courtesy Musée des Beaux-Arts, Nantes, photographed by Giraudon, Paris. 1-5: Artwork by John Jude Palencar. 6, 7: Artwork by Mark Langeneckert. 8: Detail from *Triumph of Death*, Pieter Bruegel the Elder, courtesy Museo del Prado, photographed by Robert Royal, Madrid. 10, 11: Artwork by Scott Reynolds. 12: Artwork by Rick McCollum. 15: Artwork by Chris Van Allsburg. 16-23: Artwork by Mark Langeneckert. 24: Pieter Bruegel the Elder, courtesy Museo del Prado, photographed by Robert Royal, Madrid. 25: *Death and the Miser*, Hieronymus Bosch, courtesy National Gallery of Art, Washington, Samuel H. Kress Collection, 1952. 26, 27: Herbert Arnold, courtesy Archiv für Kunst und Geschichte, West Berlin. 28: Pieter Bruegel the Elder, courtesy Museo del Prado, photographed by Robert Royal, Madrid. 29: Artwork by Stan Hunter. 30: Pieter Bruegel the Elder, courtesy Museo del Prado, photographed by Robert Royal, Madrid. 32-37: Artwork by Gary Kelley. 38, 39: Artwork by Marshall Arisman. 42, 43: Artwork by Stan Hunter. 44, 45: Artwork by Winslow Pinney Pels. 46-49: Artwork by Chris Van Allsburg. 51: Kuniyoshi, courtesy B. W. Robinson Collection, photographed by Eileen Tweedy, London. 52: Hokusai, courtesy British Museum, London, No. 1921 5-11 015. 53-55: Kuniyoshi, courtesy B. W. Robinson Collection, photographed by Eileen Tweedy, London. 57: Artwork by Yvonne Gilbert. 58, 59: Artwork by John Jude Palencar. 60: Artwork by Chris Van Allsburg. 62-69: Artwork by John Collier. 70-73: Artwork by James C. Christensen. 75: Artwork by Judy King-Rieniets. 76, 77: Artwork by Marshall Arisman. 79, 80: Artwork by Robert Goldstrom. 83: Artwork by Judy King-Rieniets. 85-90: Artwork by Brian McCall. 94, 95: Artwork by Kinuko Y. Craft. 98: Artwork by Rick McCollum. 100-107: Artwork by Chris Van Allsburg. 108-109: Artwork by Yvonne Gilbert. 111: Artwork by Marshall Arisman. 112: Artwork by Yvonne Gilbert. 115: Artwork by Kinuko Y. Craft. 116-119: Artwork by Brian McCall. 120-123: Artwork by Gary Kelley. 125: Artwork by John Collier. 126, 127: Artwork by Stan Hunter. 129-131: Artwork by Judy King-Rieniets. 132-139: Artwork by Marshall Arisman. 144: Artwork by John Jude Palencar.

TIME-LIFE BOOKS

EUROPEAN EDITOR: Kit van Tulleken
Assistant European Editor: Gillian Moore
Design Director: Ed Skyner
Photography Director: Pamela Marke
Chief of Research: Vanessa Kramer
Chief Sub-Editor: Ilse Gray

THE ENCHANTED WORLD

SERIES DIRECTOR: Ellen Phillips
Deputy Editor: Robin Richman
Designer: Dale Pollekoff
Chief Researcher: Jane Edwin

Editorial Staff for *Ghosts*
Text Editors: Tim Appenzeller,
David S. Thomson
Researchers: Patricia N. McKinney
(principal),
Charlotte Marine Fullerton
Assistant Designer: Lorraine D. Rivard
Copy Coordinators: Anthony K. Pordes,
Barbara Fairchild Quarmby
Picture Coordinator: Nancy C. Scott
Editorial Assistant: Constance B. Strawbridge

Special Contributor: Champ Clark

Correspondents: Elisabeth Kraemer-Singh
(Bonn); Margot Hapgood, Dorothy Bacon
(London); Miriam Hsia (New York); Maria
Vincenza Aloisi, Josephine du Brusle
(Paris); Ann Natanson (Rome).
Valuable assistance was also provided by:
Lois Lorimer (Copenhagen); Trini Bandrés
(Madrid); Dag Christensen (Oslo); Bogi
Augustsson (Reykjavik); Ann Wise (Rome).

Editorial Production
Chief: Jane Hawker
Art Department: Deborah Martindale
Production Assistant: Alan Godwin
Editorial Department: Theresa John,
Debra Lelliott

ISBN 7054 0883 3

Chief Series Consultant

Tristram Potter Coffin, Professor of
English at the University of Pennsylvania,
is a leading authority on folklore. He is the
author or editor of numerous books and
more than 100 articles. His best-known
works are *The British Traditional Ballad in
North America, The Old Ball Game, The Book of
Christmas Folklore* and *The Female Hero.*

This volume is one of a series that is based
on myths, legends and folk tales.